de Chirico

HARRY N. ABRAMS, INC. PUBLISHERS—NEW YORK

de Chirico

text by Isabella Far

TRANSLATED FROM FRENCH BY JOSEPH M. BERNSTEIN

Standard Book Number: 8019–0065–3
Library of Congress Catalogue Card Number: 76–83173
Copyright 1968 in Italy by Fratelli Fabbri Editori, Milan
Harry N. Abrams, Incorporated, New York
Printed and bound in Italy

In writing about the paintings and personality of Giorgio de Chirico, I realize that it is not the usual practice for a wife to present a study of her husband. Yet I feel quite qualified to do so. For years I have closely observed his evolution as an artist; I have followed with intense interest his long and arduous efforts to achieve excellence in painting and to paint in a way that resembles neither modern nor academic art. The pictures of Giorgio de Chirico exist on another level, the high level of quality, and this is the chief purpose of painting.

He has always revered the Old Masters, who succeeded in creating masterpieces because they possessed a thorough knowledge of painting, mastery of drawing, and superb craftsmanship. The Old Masters understood the nature of the pictorial medium which, over the course of generations, painters in the grand tradition have continued to improve. It is in this medium, a fundamental and indispensable element in painting, that their pictures are painted: oily, fluid, and transparent, it forms a dense, compact, and resistant body. This medium is an extremely pliable substance that helps the artist to blend colors, to model, and to paint freely. The consummate modeling gives volume and relief to the painted figures and objects; and the mysterious power characteristic of high-quality paintings in this medium suggests depth, gives a sense of space and of circulating air, and a feeling of the atmosphere that envelops figures and objects. This extraordinary blending of colors, the modeling, and the skillful use of chiaroscuro create such plasticity that the painted figures seem to be turning; they turn enough for the viewer to imagine he is seeing the side of the object that is invisible to the eye. Only paintings of great artistry—the creations of masters—have this clearly defined, compelling plasticity.

Giorgio de Chirico was aware of the difficulty for a painter of our time to try to uncover the secrets of the Old Masters. Nevertheless, he tirelessly pursued his research and continued to experiment, working constantly for improvement. An intuitive sense of painting and an immediate grasp of the techniques available to him, a feeling for his medium and an instinctive skill in using it to achieve his desired results—in short, that special understanding which an artist has of his art—all these form part of De Chirico's undeniable talent.

De Chirico's work has yielded significant, perhaps even surprising results for the age in which we live. He has succeeded in bridging the deep gap that separates the painting of our time from that of the grand tradition. The pictorial quality of his works links them to those of the great masters of the *siècles d'or*. This bond is an incontrovertible fact, unique, extraordinary, and of great importance for our century of artistic decadence.

I knew De Chirico in Paris when he was painting pictures of horses, gladiatorial combats, furniture in a valley or within a room, bits of landscape with trees whose strong roots emerging from the soil and massive trunks attested to their venerable age. He also represented seated mannequins, such as *The Archaeologists*. In all these paintings his imagination was at work, creating themes that were uniquely his own. Yet, during that same period in which he was mainly interested in what we now call "invented" pictures, he was also painting female nudes, for he had never relinquished his interest in the substance and materials of painting. Earlier, this interest had impelled him to copy paintings by Raphael (*The Pregnant Woman*), Michelangelo (*The Holy Family*), and other Masters. Not only were these copies faithful, but they came very close in pictorial quality to the famous originals.

De Chirico has always felt that painting the human body—a purely pictorial problem—is an excellent training ground for judging the validity of a medium and a technique. He painted women seated on a beach against an ocean background. In painting these nudes, he used a rather special technique. These pictures were done using an oily medium on a canvas he prepared in his studio according to a special formula. They were painted with small brush strokes that produce an effect of vibration: the white body of the woman seated in the foreground is enlivened by this special play of the brush. Light tones are used, only slightly colored, while the frequent use of white heightens the luminous effect. This technique resembles the one employed by Renoir in his later years: he too painted figures and female nudes with tiny brush strokes, in tones ranging chiefly from pink to red—thus lending unusual charm to his canvases. This kind of painting was unlike that of the Impressionists, the Expressionists, or the schools and movements that arose toward the close of the nineteenth century, when artists preached and proclaimed numerous theories as they sought to find a new way of painting. (Was this by conviction or, more probably, due to forces beyond their control? One cannot say.) In any event, De Chirico adopted for a rather brief period that technique and specific manner of painting which had been used by Renoir, not only in nudes and female figures but also in landscapes and other subjects. But in De Chirico's work, this technique is limited to a series of nudes and still lifes in which, moreover, the technique is not at all the same. Moreover, the techniques of Renoir and De Chirico are not identical. There are, however, certain aspects in common that lead me to suppose that the two painters used somewhat similar ingredients and prepared their canvases in somewhat the same way. Hence the specific manner of applying color to the canvas by means of tiny brush strokes. Though this technique of painting yields the positive qualities of luminosity, vibration, and plasticity, and produces an admittedly lovely picture, the final result is limited; for it lacks that sense of the universal, absolute, and eternal, present in the painting of the Masters.

(2

De Chirico's pictures are imbued with his love of classical antiquity which, even if he is unwilling to admit it, Greece has inspired in him. He was born in Greece and there spent his childhood and youth until the age of sixteen. The atmosphere of our early years—the blend of impressions, sensations, and fantasies we absorb—leaves an indelible imprint on every one of us. So steeped in Greek mythology was De Chirico's mind that the real and the unreal no longer possessed well-defined boundaries for him. Legends were as near and familiar to him as memories of his childhood room, where he lived with his brother Andrea and played and dreamed. But to an artist these familiar, intimate legends are much more beautiful than reality; hence he prefers them. The country in which we are born always has a special beauty; we love it tenderly, naturally, almost without awareness, the way we love the things that belong to us and are part of us. But when that country is Greece, and one is an artist, it is a special mark of good fortune to have known in childhood the light, harmony, and symmetry that are Greece. It is therefore only natural that henceforth one should never cease to draw one's inspiration from that source.

De Chirico's pictures showing two horses at the edge of the sea met with widespread public acclaim. The horses are painted with long sweeping tails and wavy manes that fall gracefully about their necks, with an occasional loose strand fluttering in the air or resting on their foreheads. Viewers were fascinated by the regal richness of these manes and of the tails that touch the ground, by the power and beauty of these magnificent animals drawing up their bodies to their full height. Here is an astonishing vision of dream horses on some legendary beach of ancient Greece. The color of the sea, a blue lightly tinged with green, is heightened by the white foam of the waves.

Here too is a deserted beach strewn with fragments of shattered columns and, on surrounding hills, temples with pure and stately lines. The temples, dedicated to the gods of Hellas, stand against the transparent sky; delicately colored with fluffy white clouds, the sky is low, near at hand, close to the earth, close to us. There is a serene and wonderful harmony in these paintings, a balanced harmony beyond anguish and desire, in which the soul finds rest and solace. Lured by the beauty of myths we hold so dear, our imagination wanders in an enchanted world of divine and human mythology. This harmony—flawless, complete—should make clear to us that the gods of mythology could not have indulged in the sordid, confused passions men have attributed to them. Actually, the gods and half-gods were human only in appearance—in reality they represented the ideal.

The·Superman, the ideal man of exalted and glorified Nature—this is the age-old dream of solitary madmen and of the more dangerous ones who combine to form mysterious and clandestine societies. The members of these secret societies are individuals who, with inflamed passion, seek their ideal in the master race, the breed of lords of the earth to which they believe they belong, and which, in their opinion, existed formerly and will exist again on the earth. They turn to paleontology and to the palingenetic theory, rearranged to suit their own purposes, in order to persuade themselves and others of the truth of their faith. De Chirico had a "revelation" when he conceived these horses which seem to have been sent down by the Muses from Mount Parnassus. This impression of semidivinity is reinforced by the luminosity of their bodies—particularly that of the horse painted in the foreground—which appear to radiate light. In certain paintings this radiation is so intense that one might think there were an electric light bulb behind the horse, flooding its body with light and surrounding it with a gleaming aura.

The first time I saw these paintings of horses I had not yet met De Chirico. At that time I did not have the understanding of painting I now have, but I did have a feeling for art and an intuitive sense for the essence of painting. The understanding of painting, like the understanding of art in general, is an innate gift. With the passage of time, one's comprehension develops, broadens, becomes surer and more complete. And only when you truly understand painting do you begin to realize how impenetrable its secrets are. There is mystery in the creation of great art: a beautiful picture is not merely an image, but a representation of an existence, a life, a world. It is an idealized reality—idealized by the creator's art. Of course, the word "reality," as related to art, is not highly thought of among avant-garde intellectuals, and this has been so for a long time. Contempt for reality and a total misunderstanding of what it represents in art are the hallmarks of our age. This point of view began to develop toward the end of the last century, when painting had become decadent and there were no more great masters. The "modern spirit" was born, with its flood of theories, trends, and new schools. This modern spirit built an entirely new framework, advancing words and phrases that distorted the meaning of many concepts, beliefs, and images that far-ranging minds had developed earlier. To these new prophets even the mementos of our dying culture were intolerable. What concerned them most was to destroy. And they have succeeded very well in their efforts. But what have they managed to build? Thus, one of their *bêtes noires* has been reality in art. I must admit—in partial justification—that painting was confused and disoriented because there were no important artists sufficiently talented and strong-willed to face up to the real as well as the unreal, and who were prepared to go about their business without worrying about which school of art they belonged to.

Besides, reality and painting are two different things; hence the futility of the modernists' concern. It is not reality but representation that matters in art. In this sense one may speak of idealized reality, which no longer draws on the wellsprings of truth but on those of beauty. All the negative, destructive speeches about reality that modern intellectuals are so fond of making have resulted, unfortunately, in confusing the mind of the average man. The latter no longer knows the reality of the concrete, no longer sees that wisdom lies in knowing a reality identified with truth, is no longer convinced that this reality is of prime importance in our lives. Just as truth is essential in the reality of life, so in painting the most important thing is the creation of the work of art. So when I discovered creative works of art —masterpieces—I was imbued with the desire to "understand" them. Moreover, I wanted to know not only the spiritual side of painting but also the other side, that of "superior craftsmanship," which struck me as equally impressive and without which great paintings would never have been possible.

Then began my frequent visits to museums. There is only one way to understand pictures: concentrate and look at them. Obviously, this method is valid only for persons who have a feeling for art. The others had better give up. If you have doubts or anxieties, that is a bad sign. When I saw De Chirico's pictures, I already had something of a background for evaluating them. As I returned time and again to the horses he painted, I let myself be carried away by the legendary atmosphere of antique gods and relived the fascinating myths of ancient Greece. At the same time I also saw the fluidity of his brush strokes, the transparency of his painting, and the sureness of his drawing. For it is only by knowledge and mastery of his craft that a painter who has forged so new and personal an aesthetic style can express it on canvas.

(4

Another favorite theme of De Chirico's was that of gladiators fighting each other, usually in an enclosed room. He often chose this setting for his pictures, because he felt at home in a room just as he felt at home, in his element, in the world of antiquity. This feeling probably arose from recollections of his childhood. His gladiators are figures which represent a fusion of statue and human being, unreal persons who were part of his metaphysical aesthetic. Frequently, before painting them on the canvas, he would draw their heads or faces in the dark, or with his eyes shut, thus letting himself be guided by his faith in the subconscious workings of his metaphysic. His gladiators have slender bodies, with well-developed muscles set sharply and even harshly in relief by deep shadows. Their hair and beards, rendered in a mass of dense, closely bunched curls, are very similar to those of the athletes of classical times. Many ancient statues of athletes have come down to us, for in ancient Greece and Rome, where the human body was the virtual object of a cult, sculptors turned to athletes as a favorite theme. The gladiators' faces are either featureless and oval-shaped, or else covered by masks like those usually worn by Roman gladiators and topped by helmets. These masked figures are often painted in a darker color, grayish in tone. When De Chirico does give features to his gladiators' faces, they are distorted and elongated. The faces of these figures, very different from one another, exemplify an aesthetic code which, as he once wrote, endowed him with clear-sightedness in painting and enabled him to build a new metaphysical psychology of things.

To afford the reader a better insight into the atmosphere of these pictures, let me quote a few lines from De Chirico's book, *Hebdomeros,* in which he reminisces about his gladiators:

"Here we are!" said Hebdomeros, extending his arms in front of his comrades in the classic gesture of a cautious captain checking the onrush of his men. They had come to the threshold of a vast, high-ceilinged hall, decorated in 1880 style. Bare of furniture, this room, in its lighting and general tone, reminded one of the gaming halls of Monte Carlo. In a corner two gladiators, wearing divers' masks, were training perfunctorily before the bored gaze of a retired master gladiator with eagle eyes and a scar-covered body. "Gladiator! this word contains an enigma," Hebdomeros murmured as he turned to the youngest of his companions. And he thought of the music hall whose illuminated ceiling evoked visions of a Dantesque Paradise; he thought too of the afternoons in Rome when, at the end of the spectacle, the sun sinks and the huge awning lengthens the shadows over the arena, and there arises a smell of sawdust and of blood-soaked sand:

Vision of Rome, ancient freshness,
Evening anguish, song of the sea.

The desire to paint pictures of furniture in a valley came to him by chance. Once, while driving on a country road, De Chirico saw some pieces of furniture lying abandoned in the fields. The unpretentious, nondescript articles, lying there with not a single living soul around, seemed bathed in an air of sadness. It was the sort of furniture one sees in households where life, too, is simple and humdrum. This strange sight of things found outside their environment, away from their usual place, provokes in us a sense of disorientation—a kind of dissociation between our habitual image of things and their sudden, unexpected appearance elsewhere. The sensitive artist intuitively grasps the poetic essence of this different atmosphere.

On his canvases the painter expresses this poetic essence as it emanates from humble objects. Because he has insight into the life of inanimate things he is able to feel this new emotion, which is basically one of quiet sadness. These purely random impressions that De Chirico received then created a counterpart in his imagination, a contrasting sensation that was more joyful and more theatrical, and that could only be realized on canvas or as part of a stage set. Haunted by this idea, he painted bits of landscape, trees, brooks, rocks, and temples in a room. The floors of these rooms are made up of long wooden slats—a motif that occurs frequently in his pictures—and fragments of columns lie there as if strewn on his legendary beaches.

De Chirico's *Seated Mannequins* and *The Archaeologists* only dimly evoke visions of Greece in their proportions, but they often contain elements of a favorite theme—columns and temples. These mannequin figures have very special proportions, with an aesthetic and a harmony all their own. One day De Chirico told me that the idea for these curious figures had come to him in a Gothic cathedral. The voices of the imagination are unpredictable, its twists and turns unforeseeable. The seated mannequins, fascinating in their strangeness, are very powerful, almost monumental, in the upper part of their bodies. But despite the weight of their torsos, their legs are short and quite thin, and their tiny feet are virtually nonexistent. There is unerring logic in the artist's depiction of these monumentlike figures. Legs and feet serve no useful purpose on monuments. But the chests of these mannequins seated next to each other are loaded with countless things taken from nature, ancient Greece, or the imagination. Their egg-shaped heads and oval faces, modeled by a deft use of light and shadow in such a way as to give their featureless faces the required plasticity, fulfill the perfect logic of this composition.

De Chirico did not define his paintings of mannequins as metaphysical, although with his *Archaeologists,* he achieved the formula that forms the basis for his metaphysical aesthetic: a meticulously calculated and deliberate use of surfaces and volumes.

(6

The period of De Chirico's "metaphysical" paintings began in 1910. A painter's mind and brain, indeed, the entire mechanism of his thinking and perception, are different and function differently from those of a philosopher, writer, musician, scientist, or any other creative person. I am talking about those few human beings who are examples of Universal Genius—for Genius exists as a thing in itself, just as talent, intelligence, and other examples of the Higher Spirit exist in the world. The human brain is aware of their existence and marvelous presence on earth. We should be grateful for having these presences among us, without attempting to explore their source. Their origins lie hidden in inscrutable mystery, in regions inaccessible to our brain.

The mental effort that goes on in a painter's brain is almost always preceded by a visual impression. *Something seen* is at the basis of his thoughts and sets his creative impulse in motion before he reproduces on his canvas what he has seen. A painter *sees* poetry, lyricism, nostalgia; he sees first of all with his eyes and only then does he feel and react. One may say that his sentiments are actually images and not emotional reactions. His eyes are the prime movers that stimulate his brain to react.

De Chirico had read Nietzsche, Weininger, and Schopenhauer, but he had *seen* the architecture of the cities of Italy—the houses with their porticoes, the public squares with their fountains and statues, the parks, streets, and railway stations. He saw and understood what Schopenhauer had meant when that German philosopher advised his fellow countrymen not to place the statues of their famous men on high columns or pedestals, but on low plinths, "as they do in Italy, where some marble men seem to be on a level with the passersby and seem to walk beside them." De Chirico used to say that he found in the architecture of Italian cities and public squares the initial inspiration for his important metaphysical aesthetic. Yet, though he had given much thought to the problem of the metaphysics of Italian architecture, the psychological origin of those Italian buildings had remained obscure to him. At the same time he asserted that all his painting during the years 1910–14 was a direct function of the sensations and emotions the cities of Italy had inspired in him. Now the enigma of that special metaphysical atmosphere, which he alone was able to glimpse and to re-create on canvas, was revealed to him. Deeply absorbed in thought, he discovered in that period of his life the metaphysical essence of Italian architecture; and his first revelation of it, as he crossed the threshold of the metaphysical world, was his unusual series of pictures of Italian squares.

In these haunting squares, the buildings are suffused with mystery and premonition. The porticoed houses, with closed shutters and corners concealing dark secrets, cast long shadows beneath a sun fading slowly in the dusk. One has the impression that something is about to happen. In the center of the square a statue of the sleeping Ariadne, a symbol of Greek art, rests on a low pedestal and is in perfect harmony with the serene atmosphere that is created despite a sense of loneliness and expectation. These visions are no longer confined to a scene represented on canvas; the painted environment participates in the vital cosmic drama where the enigmas of existence, purified and stripped of their frightening aspects, now bear the calm consoling look of the infinite. In De Chirico's view, "the absence of man is an inevitable condition, a requirement of the appearance of the metaphysical world." And, indeed, human figures are always very small, even unimportant, in his paintings of Italian squares, thus confirming this absence. De Chirico stated that one must give thought to this curious phenomenon of human absence in the metaphysical sphere, facing the fact that some questions admit of no answer. We know that entering the metaphysical world is a privilege allowed only to few. But even our intelligence, unaided, forces us daily to note and think about this absence of humanity.

During this period of his life De Chirico wrote:

One must have absolute awareness of the space an object should occupy in a picture, and understand the distance that should separate one object from another. In architecture, one must also have an absolute awareness of the space the various architectural elements in a monument should occupy, and reckon the distance that should separate them.

These words of the artist show how important the measurement of distances and the distribution of planes in the composition were to him.

De Chirico's reflections led him back to the bases of art: equilibrium and harmony. Though the paths be different, the bases remain the same, in aesthetics as well as in metaphysics.

De Chirico also painted other "revealed" pictures. Here let me quote some lines he wrote which, in a sense, explain the source of those rather strange subjects he called "Metaphysical Interiors." For centuries geometrical figures have represented, in some fields, symbols of higher reality. The triangle, for example, served as a symbol for various beliefs, age-old superstitions, and even secret societies. Even today theosophy uses it as a mystic and magic symbol.

The triangle often arouses in an individual who looks at it, even when he does not know its traditional meaning, a feeling of anxiety and even fear. Thus, rules, squares, and compasses—the tools of geometry—used to haunt and still haunt my mind. I still see them appearing like mysterious stars and rising up behind each of my pictorial creations.

As early as the 1910–14 period the artist expressed himself in the following terms:

The question of Innocence: there are men who do not know the *terror* inherent in signs and angles, and yet they are borne toward infinity. Thus is revealed their limited mind, enclosed within the same circle, like the mind of a child or woman. But we who know the signs of the metaphysical alphabet know what joys and sorrows are contained in a portico, a street corner, a room, on a table top, or between the sides of a box. We know, and we are building in painting the new metaphysical psychology of things. The philosopher Otto Weininger has made a profound comment on the metaphysical art of geometry: "The angle of the circle may be beautiful as ornament, but that does not mean its perfect completion—or that, like the Midgard Serpent encircling the world, it is no longer vulnerable to criticism."

(8

Such were the mental speculations that strongly influenced De Chirico, who used painting to explain to himself sensations he could not translate into words.

De Chirico's writings at this time were the product of an intellectual and artistic world in revolution. The revolution may not have been a bloody one; but at the very least it was extremely turbulent and noisy. Avant-garde groups hoisted banners representing the most diverse points of view. People wrote, thought—and shouted. Yet this deafening noise was produced by persons who still had ideals. True or false ideals? What did it matter! Dying idealism thus sang, like a white swan, its death song. De Chirico and his brother plunged into intellectual speculations, read the German philosophers, pondered, and wrote down their thoughts as they sought to explain their ideas.

Impelled by the desire to communicate his dreams, De Chirico painted his metaphysical interiors. It was as if he were gathering up his visions, reduced to a small format, and enclosing them in a room. Time and again he used a room as the setting for his most hallucinating visions, because he liked the security of a room. Thus, in one room was a collection of boxes that contained landscapes; there were angles, cubes, surfaces, and triangles, on which were traced geometrical signs and figures of the metaphysics Weininger and he had deeply probed. There were also biscuits, lending a familiar yet mysterious note in that setting. Sometimes he would paint a house, a temple, or a fountain in the landscapes depicted on the boxes. So in these interiors, for all to see, appeared the geometer's rules and compasses that had haunted him and that, as he confessed, he saw behind all his pictorial creations.

Other visions of his metaphysical world came to life on his canvases—startling, unexpected apparitions beyond our usual ken. The *Disquieting Muses* opened a curtain and ushered in mysterious figures reminiscent of the *Mannequins.* They held an important place in the artist's metaphysical world, and their appearance on the pictures of Italian squares could have been anticipated. The same atmosphere—the same *Stimmung*—surrounds these figures; but now they are in the foreground. De Chirico painted these enigmatic beings at the same time that he presented his *Troubadour,* a strange poetic figure standing alone in the center of the canvas. The backgrounds, colored in the same tones as those of the Italian squares, reveal very low and distant horizons. Two sections of walls, or sometimes a view of a portico, usually rise on both sides of the figures—in the *Troubadour* paintings as well as in those depicting Hector and Andromache. The Troubadour, to us the embodiment of medieval poetry, seems to be invoked here as the originator of a new metaphysical poetry.

On other canvases appear two of his mystery figures: side by side, joined in indissoluble harmony, they rekindle memories of the Hector-Andromache myth, the symbol of ideal married love and of the lofty emotions felt by persons of unusual moral stature. For Hector and Andromache as metaphysical mannequins, was there a different make-up of heart and soul in their inner being? Perhaps it was in the geometrical shapes by which they were surrounded and supported: fantastically shaped squares, rods, and triangles with openings in circular form and crisscrossed by lines.

We have grown increasingly familiar with these metaphysical mannequins, although "familiar" is perhaps not the right word. It is not they who come closer to us; we come closer to them. At present we know that in our everyday life, whether indoors or on the street, we meet figures disguised as human beings. It takes skill to recognize them; and now no mask can hide them from us.

De Chirico's inner life as an artist reached its high point during periods in which he was under the sway of his visions, revelations, inspirations, and desires. The thick curtain separating this other world from our own, where so many things remain to be discovered, opened before the artist, leaving his mind free to turn toward the realm of great art. During these periods he thought about painting and was inspired in a different way. Now he spent much of his time visiting museums. Above all, he engaged in research, experiments, and exercises, in a never-ending effort to discover the road on which he would find the key to great painting.

During the periods of insight and revelation, he painted "invented" pictures such as *The Mysterious Baths,* in which the bathers' stalls are set on raised platforms with wooden floors; from the water below emerge the nude torsos of curly-headed adolescents. These bathers remind one of the marble statues of athletes, those men of stone who, to the artist, are part of the "second aspect" of men, nature, and things. This second aspect often permitted De Chirico to see things not visible to our eyes; manifested on his canvases and intimately bound up with his personality, this "second sight" created a strange, indefinable atmosphere, neither dream world nor reality.

He painted short, squat warriors covered with a peplum and wearing a legionary's helmet adorned with large, vividly colored feathers. These warriors contrast in stature with the tall, long-faced gladiators. In addition, the whole conception of the painting is different. Yet these canvases give one a sense of harmony and serenity.

The artist also painted women hiding behind curtains and screens, showing only glimpses of their mysterious faces and Amazonian hair. But he rarely dealt with these themes.

Despite his interest in the world on the other side of the curtain and the figures who inhabited it, De Chirico's passion for beauty in painting and for the absolute values of art grew ever stronger in him. I recall one incident. One day we were in a museum, and he was making a close analysis of a famous painting, when suddenly he exclaimed: "Only with material like this can one paint!" He meant true painting, great painting, where there is also an *aspect* of reality—a higher and idealized reality.

Like an alchemist in his laboratory, De Chirico spent whole days and sometimes even nights searching for the wonder-working substance, mixing ingredients which, he thought, composed it. The great problem—and the great mystery—was the ingredients and the exact amount of each. Did a painter have to work like an alchemist, become a kind of magician and spend his precious time looking for the emulsion or paste which, when mixed with the colors, would give body to the painting and enable him to model with the ease and freedom displayed in pictures of the great masters? What cruel fate has deprived artists of the very basic concepts of a body of knowledge as complicated as painting? Once those ideas were elementary and familiar even to second-rate painters. They knew at least the alphabet and grammar of their craft and would not settle for the pseudo knowledge that now pretends to be craft.

It was essential for De Chirico to discover a consistent, easy-to-handle material in which color was used only for coloring and not for the very body of the painting. He passed through various stages before reaching the point at which he could paint pictures that satisfied him and were good enough to become part of the great tradition in painting. First of all, he had to discover the principle of a pliable material—an emulsion, soft paste, or oil substance—that would enable him to create a strong, tightly knit pictorial web. Next he had to find the various elements that made up this material. This required long, difficult, and painstaking research, but the outcome was successful, and he was able to resume the tradition of the Old Masters and to create paintings of genuine artistic worth. If we want painting to continue as a great plastic art, an art that for centuries has given us priceless masterpieces, we must rediscover and restudy the science of painting, a body of knowledge that has been completely forgotten.

Giorgio de Chirico has always had a love of painting. Even in his youth he produced beautiful pictures. A period of "invented" canvases was followed by a period in which a kind of daemon of art seized him. But the techniques he had used no longer satisfied him when he attained artistic maturity. He was attracted by free painting. The development of great painting demonstrates that for the artist, including those who flourished in the great periods of painting, the high point was free painting in which the artist's mastery was given full sway. Paintings were no longer a set of statistical data but mysteriously living, vibrating things on canvas. Thanks to their plasticity and relief, figures and objects *turn,* as Renoir used to say.

On De Chirico's canvases air circulates, horizons recede, textures are supple, nature becomes magical. No longer is there anything ugly or harsh, for his pictures portray the reality that only true art can idealize.

Men of our time generally see only the depicted scene in an old or a modern painting: they see landscapes, figures of men or women, a street with houses, flowers and fruit—in short, objects of all kinds treated in a more or less naturalistic manner, and more or less clearly rendered. Modern men also see in contemporary painting motifs, touches of color, lines, abstract forms . . . in sum, the subjects represented in abstract paintings. The public is not surprised to see objects and figures broken down or distorted, because the modern eye is used to distortion. But above all, it is the subject of a painting that people see, as if a painting were simply an image and not a work of art. Nowadays most people consider paintings an element of decoration. To others, more intellectually inclined, the painting is an image, a representation conceived by the painter's mind. In such canvases they see ideas, intentions, expressions of the mind, and, of course, many other things as well—but all of them of an intellectual nature. Nevertheless, I repeat, we are still talking about the same thing: it is the subject—whether image or representation —which remains the thing modern man sees, perceives, or thinks about. He no longer understands the higher meaning of art; whether the painting be a mediocre one or a masterpiece, to him it is summed up in an image. When he knows that a painting is recognized as a masterpiece, he accepts it as such without seeing or understanding the true meaning and artistic superiority of the work.

Actually, in painting it is much harder to grasp the metaphysical aspects of the painting as painting than it is to understand such aspects inherent in the subject matter. It is far easier to grasp the essence of a mood, an atmosphere, a startling and mysterious "tone." It is not that one really *understands,* but one realizes that there is something *more,* something *different* in a given painting; and one's intelligence and insight are flattered at having discovered this "something." Of course it is hard to understand the real meaning of De Chirico's "metaphysical" and "invented" pictures, or of Picasso's paintings, which, according to Picasso himself, convey the essence of figures and objects. This essence is preserved, regardless of any distortion or fragmentation. Similarly, in some of his works Picasso preserves the ironical aspect of things as well as their peculiar, melancholy poetry.

But to feel and understand the phenomenon of art in all its overpowering greatness transcends the work of the brain: it is a gift, a revelation to the human spirit from on high. To simple people who look at a work of art in their simple, uncomplicated way, the pure pleasure and admiration they feel lifts them above their everyday life. It is a kind of manna falling from heaven, which they, in their simplicity, appreciate. To a student or lover of art, but especially to a great artist, a masterpiece is a thing of joy, a revelation, a passionate communion with the higher phenomenon of art that towers above our earthbound intellectual speculations and analyses.

The very fine reproductions of De Chirico's paintings assembled in this volume show the wide range of his subjects. Here you will see Perseus speeding on a winged horse to free Ariadne; naiads in a stream in the midst of an enchanted forest; horses with colored, fluttering trappings; fruit set against a landscape with far-off horizons; a large still life where, on a richly furnished table with a tablecloth of brocade, a head of Minerva is surrounded by roses, grapes, and other ripe fruit, flanked by curtains. Balancing the Minerva, a head of Apollo appears in the center of the canvas on a table covered by a white cloth. Not far away is a thick book bound in dark red leather resting on a very bright green hanging. The latter harmonizes in tone with the silver goblet, ewer, and tureen that reflect, as in a mirror, the objects painted on the canvas. You will see scenes of Venice, imaginary landscapes with knights, and the scenes from Greek mythology that are so close to the artist's personality. The subjects of these paintings vary widely, but all of them have in common an excellence in drawing and modeling, great plasticity of form, beauty of substance, and carefully balanced composition—and they are all bathed in an airy, transparent, and luminous atmosphere. In short, these pictures possess the essential qualities that only great painting can have.

When Giorgio de Chirico sits down at his easel and begins to paint a picture, he chooses the subject that interests and attracts him that day. Sometimes he is impelled to paint a scene with figures from ancient Greece, gods or demigods; sometimes he chooses pieces of fruit or horses. At his easel the painter feels his power and says, like the French kings of old: "Such is our pleasure." Thus he paints what he wants to paint, with the freedom and mastery he has always sought to achieve. Now, having been well guided by his Muse, he has achieved his goal.

Giorgio de Chirico loves painting. It is his great passion. His devotion to art and his consciousness of his mission may be summed up in his own words:

As for myself, I am serene and lay proud claim to the three words I should like to have as the seal set on each of my works: *Pictor classicus sum* (I am a classical painter).

Biographical Sketch of Giorgio de Chirico

Giorgio de Chirico was born in 1888 in Volos, capital of Thessaly. His parents, natives of Italy, were living in Greece at that time because his father, an engineer, was employed by a Thessalian company engaged in railroad construction. The painter was born in a villa surrounded by a garden, on a very hot day in July.

From his earliest years De Chirico showed an aptitude for painting. As soon as he was able to hold a pencil in his hand, he began to draw everything that passed through his fingers. Acquiring some proficiency in drawing, young De Chirico took special delight in copying illustrations from the French *L'Illustration* and other magazines to which his parents subscribed. He copied pictures of famous men and noted artists reproduced in these magazines; he also sketched ordinary objects that caught his attention. The budding artist kept a pencil and notebook in his pocket, and sketching was his pastime, his favorite game. This passion for drawing led him to observe closely everything around him. Little by little he began to see things with the eye of a painter.

He spent his childhood and early youth in Athens. He studied at first with a Greek drawing teacher named Mavrudis, an intelligent and discerning man who encouraged him to make a serious study of art. Then, at the age of twelve, his father sent him to the Athens Polytechnic Institute. Thus began for De Chirico the great adventure of his life—the adventure of painting. After his father's death in 1905, De Chirico, then aged sixteen, left Greece and went to Italy, accompanied by his mother and brother. They were on their way to Munich, where the young artist wanted to continue his studies at the Academy of Fine Arts, then reputed to be one of the best in the world; however, they had decided first to visit several Italian cities.

It was in Munich that De Chirico first became interested in the Swiss painter

Arnold Böcklin. The latter's pictures exerted such a strong influence on the youthful De Chirico that the canvases he painted at that time have been described as belonging to his "Böcklin period." During that period, too, he devoted much of his time to reading the works of the German philosophers. The writings of Schopenhauer, Weininger, and especially Nietzsche deeply impressed and influenced him.

Returning to Italy in 1909, the artist lived in Milan and, in his own words, "painted Böcklinesque canvases." In 1910 he moved to Florence, where, because of poor health, he was forced to spend a great deal of time in bed. At best, he was able occasionally to paint some small canvases. Meanwhile, he continued to read and study, particularly the works of his favorite philosophers; at times he fell into moods of somber depression. The "Böcklin period" had by now ended and De Chirico was beginning to depict themes in which he sought to translate the powerful and mysterious emotions he had discovered in Nietzsche's works: the melancholy of lovely autumn days, afternoon in Italian cities. Thus were foreshadowed the themes of his "Italian Squares," which he painted later in Paris.

In 1911 De Chirico decided to join his brother Andrea in Paris. He left Florence in July of that year and traveled with his mother to the French capital, stopping for several days at Turin, the city in which Nietzsche had spent his last years. In Paris the family took an apartment and De Chirico began again to paint, resuming the thread of his Nietzsche-inspired ideas. In the artistic circles he frequented, there was much talk of the Salon d'Automne, of revolutionary painters, of Picasso, Cubism, and other modern schools of art.

A year later, on the advice of the poet Guillaume Apollinaire, De Chirico participated in the Salon d'Automne, where he exhibited a *Self-Portrait,* an *Italian Square* inspired by the Piazza Santa Croce in Florence, and a canvas titled *Enigma of the Oracle,* inspired by early Greek history. His paintings achieved some success and were praised by a number of critics. His friends advised him to exhibit at the Salon des Indépendants of 1913; he showed several paintings here and continued to participate in group exhibitions, including a second showing at the Salon d'Automne (1913).

The outbreak of war in 1914 forced De Chirico to return to Italy the following year. He was assigned to an infantry regiment in Ferrara, but eventually obtained a position as a clerk at the city's military headquarters. Thus he had off-duty hours during which to paint. This gave him an opportunity to become acquainted with one of the Italian cities that impressed him most and inspired some of his metaphysical interiors. On account of poor health, he was finally sent to a nearby hospital, where he was permitted to paint.

Soon after the end of the war, in the winter of 1918–19, De Chirico went to Rome. Here he spent much time in museums, studying the techniques and copying paintings of the Old Masters, striving to probe their secrets. For a few years (1920–22) he was interested in working in tempera, and in this medium he executed the "Roman Villa" series of paintings. During the years in Rome and after his return to Paris in 1925, he sporadically revived the themes and manner of his earlier metaphysical paintings, but most of his works of this period reflect new sources of inspiration: Renaissance, Baroque, and certain nineteenth-century masters, as well as classical antiquity. It was during the artist's second sojourn in Paris (1925–31) that he met his wife, Isabella Far.

De Chirico returned to Italy in 1931, exhibiting in Milan and various other Italian cities. In 1933 he was invited to Florence to design costumes and stage sets for Bellini's opera *I Puritani,* which was to be staged during the spring music festival—the Maggio Musicale—in that city. Then, at the Palazzo della Triennale in Milan, he did a large mural painting in egg tempera, a work that was subsequently destroyed. In 1936 he came to New York and organized a large one-man show. He remained in the United States for eighteen months. Shortly after his return to Paris, the outbreak of World War II necessitated his return to Italy; he spent the war years in Milan and Florence.

In 1948 De Chirico exhibited at the Venice Biennale. From then on he has continued to paint realistic pictures, with interludes of metaphysical and fantasy paintings. He has also designed many stage sets and costumes for the Rome Opera, La Scala in Milan, and the Florence Maggio Musicale.

Books and Articles on Giorgio de Chirico

Apollinaire, Guillaume. *Les soirées de Paris,* no. 18, November 15, 1913; no. 22, March 15, 1914 (Reviews).

Pisis, Filippe de. "Il pittore Giorgio de Chirico," *Gazzetta Ferrarese,* October 11, 1916.

———, "Carlo Carrà—G. de Chirico," *Gazzetta Ferrarese,* February 12, 1918.

———, *"Pittura Moderna": Carlo Carrà e G. de Chirico.* Ferrara, 1919.

———, "Disegni di Giorgio de Chirico," *La Provincia di Ferrara,* no. 23, February 21, 1919.

Dodici Opere di Giorgio de Chirico. Rome, Edizione Valori Plastici, 1919.

Raimondi, Giuseppe. "Giorgio de Chirico," *Il Convegno,* 1920.

Castelfranco, Giorgio. *Catalogo della Mostra Personale del Pittore Giorgo de Chirico alla Galleria "Arte"* (Preface). Milan, 1921.

Broglio, Mario. *Giorgio de Chirico* (Catalogo della Fiorentina Primaverile). Florence, 1922.

Castelfranco, Giorgio. "Giorgio de Chirico," *Jahrbuch der Jungen Kunst,* 1924.

Naville, Pierre, and Péret, Benjamin, eds. *La Révolution Surréaliste,* no. 1, December 1924.

Lissitzky, El, and Arp, Hans. *The Isms of Art.* "Chirico." Zurich, 1925.

Mandiargues, André Pieyre de. "La cité métaphisique," *Disc Vert,* no. 5, 1925.

Morise, Max. "A propos de l'exposition Chirico," *La Révolution Surréaliste,* no. 4, July 1925.

Courthion, Pierre. "Giorgio de Chirico," *Cahiers d'Art,* no. 5, June 1926.

Ribemont–Dessaignes, G. "Giorgio de Chirico," *Les Feuilles Libres,* no. 43, May–June 1926.

Barnes, Albert C. *Exposition d'oeuvres de Giorgio de Chirico chez Paul Guillaume* (Catalogue). Paris, 1926.

Carrà, Carlo. "Le arti: de Chirico," *L'Ambrosiano,* 1926.

"Le mostre individuali a Milano: Giorgio de Chirico," *Il Convegno,* April 1926.

Castelfranco, Giorgio. *Giorgio de Chirico* (Preface to the catalogue of a one-man exhibition at Galeria Pesaro). Milan, 1926.

Courthion, Pierre. *Panorama de la Peinture française contemporaine.* "Le 'Rêve,' Giorgio de Chirico." 1927.

Raynal, Maurice. *Giorgio de Chirico.* ("Anthologie de la Peinture en France de 1906 à nos jours"). Paris, 1927.

Vitrac, Roger. *Giorgio de Chirico et son oeuvre.* Paris, Gallimard, 1927.

Giedion, S. "Neue Italienische Malerei," *Der Cicerone,* 1927.

George, Waldemar. *Exposition Giorgio de Chirico à la Galerie Jean Bucher* (Catalogue). Paris, 1927.

Gibson, W. "Giorgio de Chirico," *The Enemy,* January 1927.

Tozzi, Mario. "Giorgio de Chirico," *Le Arti Plastiche,* 1927.

Ternovetz, Boris. *Giorgio de Chirico.* Milan, Hoepli, 1928.

George, Waldemar. *Chirico, avec des fragments littéraires de l'artiste.* Paris, Chroniques du Jour, 1928.

Goodrich, Lloyd. "Giorgio de Chirico," *The Arts,* January 1929.

Naville, Pierre, and Péret, Benjamin, eds. *La Révolution Surréaliste,* no. 12, December 1929.

Soffici, A. *Scoperte e massacri: de Chirico e Savinio,* 2nd edition. Florence, Vallecchi, 1929 (written in 1914; first edition 1919).

Delbanco, Gustav. "Henry Moore und Giorgio de Chirico," *Die Weltkunst,* no. 17, April 1931.

Soby, James Thrall. *The Early Chirico.* New York, Dodd, Mead, 1941.

Carrieri, Raffaele. *Giorgio de Chirico.* Milan, Garzanti, 1942.

Melville, Robert. "Rousseau and de Chirico," *Scottish Arts and Letters,* no. 1, 1944.

Breddo, Gastone. "Giorgio de Chirico, pittore surrealista," *Lettere ed Arti,* no. 1, September 1945.

Lo Duca, Giuseppe. *Dipinti de Giorgio de Chirico,* 2nd edition. Milan, Hoepli, 1945 (first edition 1936).

Gaffé, René. *Giorgio de Chirico, le voyant.* Brussels, La Boétie, 1946.

Pica, Agnoldomenico. *12 Opere di Giorgio de Chirico.* Milan, Edizione del Milione, 1947.

Apollonio, Umbro. "La pittura metafisica alla XXIV Biennale," *Le Arti Belle,* nos. 14–15, 1948.

Faldi, Italo. *Il Primo de Chirico.* Venice, Alfieri, 1949.

Collis, Maurice. "Giorgio de Chirico," *Art News and Review,* no. 8, May 1949.

Ragghianti, Carlo L. "Il Primo de Chirico," *La Critica d'Arte,* November 1949.

Alloway, Lawrence. "The Early Chirico, the London Gallery," *Art News and Review,* no. 6, April 1949.

Acqua, Gian Alberto dell'. "La peinture métaphysique," *Cahiers d'Art,* no. 25, 1950.

Far, Isabella. *Giorgio de Chirico.* Rome, Bestetti, 1953.

✓ Soby, James Thrall. *Giorgio de Chirico,* new edition. New York, The Museum of Modern Art, 1966.

1919 "Noi metafisici," *Cronache d'attualità*, Rome, February 15.

"Sull'arte metafisica," *Valori Plastici*, Rome, April–May.

1920 "Paul Gauguin," *Il Convegno*, Milan, March.

"Raffaello Sanzio," *Il Convegno*, Milan, April.

"Arnoldo Boeklin," *Il Convegno*, Milan, May.

"Classicismo pittorico," *La Ronda*, Rome, July.

"Gaetano Previati," *Il Convegno*, Milan, August.

" 'Pittura metafisica' di Carlo Carrà," *Il Convegno*, Milan, August.

"Max Klinger," *Il Convegno*, Milan, November.

"Ottone Rosai," *La Toscana della Sera*, Leghorn, December 14.

1921 "Riflessioni sulla pittura antica," *Il Convegno*, Milan, April–May.

1924 "Courbet," *Rivista di Firenze*, Florence, November.

"Un Rêve," *La Révolution Surréaliste*, Paris, December.

1925 "Vale Lutetia" (followed by an Epode), *Rivista di Firenze*, Florence, February.

"Une nuit," *La Révolution Surréaliste*, Paris, October 15.

"Courbet," *Valori Plastici*, Rome.

1927 "Statues, meubles et généraux," *Bulletin de l'Effort Moderne*, no. 38, Paris, October.

1928 *Piccolo trattato di tecnica pittorica*. Milan, Scheiwiller.

1929 *Hebdomeros, le peintre et son génie chez l'écrivain*. Paris, Éditions du Carrefour. (English edition: Translated, with an Introduction, by James A. Hodkinson. New York, Four Seasons Book Society, 1966.)

1931 "Le fils de l'ingénieur," *Poligono*, Milan, March.

1934 "Sur le silence," *Minotaure*, no. 5, Paris, May.

1938 "Mystery and Creation," *London Bulletin*, no. 6. Text in English and French.

"Barnes collezionista mistico," *L'Ambrosiano*, Milan, February 16.

"Vox clamans in deserto (I, II, III)," *L'Ambrosiano*, Milan, March 16, 23, 30.

1941 "Perché ho illustrato l'Apocalisse," *Stile*, Milan, January.

"Gregorio Sciltian," *Stile*, Milan, April.

1945 (1918–25) *Ricordi di Roma*. Rome, Editrice Cultura Moderna.

Memorie della mia vita. Rome, Astrolabio.

Commedia dell'Arte Moderna (in collaboration with Isabella Far). Rome, Nuove Edizioni Italiane.

1946 "Une nuit" (1911–13), "Une vie" (1911–13), "Espoirs" (1911–13), in Carola Giedion-Welcker, *Poètes à l'Ecart*, Bern.

Numerous other articles in journals and reviews.

List of Illustrations

In the measurements of the paintings, height precedes width.
Unless otherwise noted, paintings are in oil on canvas.

1 *The Philosopher*. 1925. $31\frac{7}{8} \times 25\frac{7}{8}''$. Collection Giovanni Traversa, Rivoli

2 *The Philosopher's Promenade*. 1914. $53 \times 25''$. Collection Vicomtesse de Noailles, Paris

3 *The Conquest of the Philosopher*. 1914. $49\frac{1}{2} \times 39\frac{1}{2}''$. The Art Institute of Chicago

4 *The Gentle Afternoon*. 1916. $25\frac{1}{4} \times 23''$. The Peggy Guggenheim Collection, Venice

5 *Turin, Spring*. 1914. $48\frac{3}{8} \times 39\frac{1}{4}''$. Collection Vicomtesse de Noailles, Paris

6 *Landscape Painter*. 1918. $39\frac{3}{8} \times 27\frac{5}{8}''$. Private collection, Turin

7 *The Departure of the Friend*. 1950. $19\frac{5}{8} \times 15\frac{3}{4}''$. Private collection, Rome

8 *Autumnal Melancholy*. 1915. $25\frac{1}{4} \times 20\frac{1}{8}''$. Collection Isabella Far, Rome

9 *The Return of the Prodigal Son*. 1924. $41\frac{3}{8} \times 27\frac{5}{8}''$. Private collection, Turin

10 *Return of the Prodigal Son*. 1965. $31\frac{1}{2} \times 23\frac{5}{8}''$. Private collection, Rome

11 *The Song of Love*. 1914. $28\frac{3}{4} \times 23\frac{1}{2}''$. Private collection, New York

12 *The Philosopher and the Poet*. 1913. Drawing, $12\frac{1}{2} \times 9\frac{1}{2}''$. Collection Roland Penrose, London (Photo J. Webb)

13 *The Philosopher and the Poet*. 1914. $32\frac{1}{4} \times 26''$. Private collection, Rome

14 *The Disquieting Muses*. 1917. $38\frac{1}{4} \times 26''$. Private collection, Milan

15 *Hector and Andromache*. 1917. $35\frac{1}{2} \times 23\frac{5}{8}''$. Private collection, Milan

16 *The Enigma of the Hour*. 1948. $15\frac{3}{4} \times 19\frac{5}{8}''$. Private collection, Rome

17 *The Great Tower*. 1914. $13 \times 13''$. Private collection, Milan

18 *Ancient Horses*. 1958. $19\frac{5}{8} \times 15\frac{3}{4}''$. Private collection, Rome

19 *Joy*. 1913. Drawing, $6\frac{1}{2} \times 8\frac{1}{2}''$. Collection Roland Penrose, London (Photo J. Webb)

20 *The Enigma of the Hour*. 1912. $21\frac{5}{8} \times 28''$. Private collection, Milan

21 *Metaphysical Interior*. 1946. $38\frac{1}{8} \times 28\frac{3}{8}''$. Private collection, Rome

22 *Metaphysical Interior*. 1965. Private collection, Rome

23 *The Child's Brain*. 1914. $31\frac{1}{2} \times 24\frac{3}{4}''$. National Museum, Stockholm

24 *The Tower*. 1918. $35\frac{3}{8} \times 13\frac{3}{4}''$. Private collection, Rome

25 *Hector and Andromache*. 1966. $27\frac{5}{8} \times 19\frac{5}{8}''$. Private collection, Rome

26 *The Soothsayer's Recompense*. 1913. $52\frac{3}{4} \times 70\frac{1}{2}''$. Philadelphia Museum of Art. Louise and Walter Arensberg Collection

27 *The Melancholy of Departure*. 1916. $19\frac{7}{8} \times 13\frac{3}{8}''$. Collection Roland Penrose, London

28 *The Grand Metaphysician*. 1917. $41\frac{1}{4} \times 27\frac{1}{2}''$. The Museum of Modern Art, New York

29 *The Uncertainty of the Poet*. 1913. $41\frac{1}{2} \times 37''$. Collection Roland Penrose, London

30 *The Mysterious Swimmer*. 1930. $23\frac{5}{8} \times 19\frac{5}{8}''$. Private collection, Turin

31 *The Mysterious Baths*. 1930. $27\frac{1}{4} \times 19\frac{5}{8}''$. Collection Monica Vitti, Rome

32 *The Mysterious Baths*. 1966. $27\frac{5}{8} \times 19\frac{5}{8}''$. Private collection, Rome

33 *Furniture in the Valley*. 1966. $39\frac{3}{8} \times 31\frac{1}{2}''$. Private collection, Rome

34 *Furniture in the Valley*. 1927. $51\frac{1}{8} \times 39\frac{3}{8}''$. Collection Franchetti, Rome

35 *The Melancholy of a Beautiful Day*. 1913. $35 \times 41\frac{7}{8}''$. Collection Benedict L. Goldschmidt, Brussels

36 *The Fatal Temple*. 1913. $13\frac{1}{8} \times 16\frac{1}{8}''$. Philadelphia Museum of Art. A. E. Gallatin Collection

37 *Mannequins at the Seashore*. 1926. $31\frac{7}{8} \times 26''$. Collection R. Morone, Turin

38 *The Comforter*. 1929. $39 \times 32\frac{1}{4}''$. Private collection, Rome

39 *The Archaeologists*. 1929. $45\frac{1}{4} \times 37\frac{3}{8}''$. Private collection, Rome

40 *The Archaeologist*. 1926–27. $37\frac{3}{4} \times 50\frac{3}{8}''$. Private collection, Milan

41 *The Painter*. 1927. Private collection, Milan

42 *The Rose Tower*. 1913. $29\frac{1}{2} \times 39\frac{1}{2}''$. The Peggy Guggenheim Collection, Venice

43 *Autumn Afternoon.* 1920. 43¼″ × 28¾″. Private collection, Rome

44 *Two Masks.* 1916. 22 × 18½″. Private collection, Milan

45 *Roman Piazza.* 1922. 22 × 29⅞″. Collection Alfredo Casella

46 *Roman Villa.* 1922. 39⅜ × 29¾″. Collection G. Bruno Pagliai, Mexico City

47 *Azure Mannequin.* 1966. Drawing, 14⅛ × 9¾″. Collection Cesare Monti, Milan

48 *The Condottiere.* 1917. Drawing, 11¼ × 8⅛″. Collection James Thrall Soby, New Canaan, Connecticut

49 *The Troubadour.* 1966. 27⅝ × 19⅝″. Private collection, Rome

50 *Morning Meditation.* 1912. 20½ × 28¾″. Collection Riccardo Jucker, Milan

51 *Thermopylae.* 1947. 19⅝ × 23⅝″. Private collection, Rome

52 *The Enigma of Fatality.* 1914. 54⅜ × 37½″. Kunstmuseum, Basel (Photo Hans Hinz)

53 *Colonial Mannequins.* 1945. 31½ × 21⅝″. Private collection, Rome

54 *Heraldic Mannequins.* 1926. 47¼ × 35⅜″. Collection Elena Sacerdoti, Milan

55 *Soothsayers.* 1966. 27⅝ × 19⅝″. Private collection, Rome

56 Copy of Raphael's *Pregnant Woman.* 1922. 25⅝ × 19¼″. Private collection, Rome

57 *Christ and the Magdalen.* 1954. 11¾ × 15¾″. Private collection, Rome

58 *Hector with His Horse Podargus.* 1966. 23⅝ × 19⅝″. Private collection, Rome

59 *Fruit and Flowers.* 1963. 43¼ × 55⅛″. Private collection, Rome

60 *Sleeping Ariadne.* 1934. Terracotta. Private collection, Rome

61 *Hector and Andromache.* 1936. Terracotta, 16⅞ × 8⅝ × 6¾″. Private collection, Chiavenna

62 *Children* (after a Flemish artist). 1956. 11¾ × 15¾″. Private collection, Rome

63 *Black Grapes and Peaches.* 1951. 15¾ × 19⅝″. Private collection, Rome

64 *Paris with Hector's Horse.* 1960. 19⅝ × 23⅝″. Private collection, Rome

65 *Fruit in a Landscape.* 1944. 15¾ × 19⅝″. Private collection, Rome

66 *Self-Portrait.* 1934. 11 × 7½″. Private collection, Rome

67 *Isabella Far.* 1935. 39⅜ × 31½″. Private collection, Rome

68 *The Fall—Station of the Way of the Cross.* 1947. Private collection, Rome

69 *Christ between the Thieves.* 1965. 31½ × 43¼″. Collection Bonfedi, Milan

70 *The Divine Horse Arion, Son of Neptune.* 1957. 19⅝ × 15¾″. Private collection, Rome

71 *Horses.* 1952. 7⅞ × 11¾″. Private collection, Rome

72 *Tulips.* 1957. 13¾ × 17¾″. Private collection, Rome

73 *The Picador.* 1935. 15 × 18⅞″. Private collection, Rome

74 *Self-Portrait at the Easel.* 1934. 51⅛ × 29½″. Private collection, Rome

75 *Lady of the Court.* 1950. 23⅝ × 19⅝″. Private collection, Rome

76 *Bathing Naiads.* 1955. 32¼ × 42½″. Private collection, Rome

77 *Horse and Zebra on the Beach of the Island of Lemnos.* 1965. 19⅝ × 27⅝″. Private collection, Rome

78 *Ancient Horse on the Shore of the Aegean.* 1966. 19⅝ × 23⅝″. Private collection, Rome

79 *Phaethon and Lampos, Horses of Eos.* 1965. 39⅜ × 31½″. Private collection, Rome

80 *The Ungulates.* 1965. 39⅜ × 31½″. Private collection, Rome

81 *Antique Serenity.* 1966. 23⅝ × 31½″. Private collection, Rome

82 *The Guardian of Thermopylae.* 1966. 23⅝ × 19⅝″. Private collection, Rome

83 *Basket with Fruit.* 1957. 15¾ × 19⅝″. Private collection, Rome

84 *Tomatoes.* 1936. 15¾ × 19⅝″. Private collection, Rome

85 *Dioscuro.* 1936. 10¼ × 7⅛″. Private collection, Rome

86 *Leda.* 1934. 19⅝ × 17¾″. Private collection, Rome

87 *Horses.* 1966. Drawing, 9⅞ × 14⅛″. Collection Vincenzo Monti, Milan

88 *Head of a Horse.* 1959. 19⅝ × 15¾″. Private collection, Rome

89 *Still Life with Copper Objects*. 1942. 20⅛ × 29⅞″. Private collection, Rome

90 *Armor*. 1953. 21⅝ × 29½″. Private collection, Rome

91 *Forest in Cascine Park, Florence*. 1933. 21⅝ × 15″. Private collection, Rome

92 *Winter*. 1940. 31½ × 23⅝″. Private collection, Rome

93 *Achilles at the Source of the Peneus*. 1961. 27⅝ × 39⅜″. Private collection, Rome

94 *Alexander the Great with His Companions*. 1958. 37⅜ × 53⅛″. Private collection, Rome

95 *Christ on the Cross*. 1951. 31½ × 26¾″. Private collection, Rome

96 *Atelier of the Master in Paris*. 1934. 22½ × 18½″. Private collection, Rome

97 *Baby, My Great Dane*. 1934. 9½ × 15¾″. Private collection, Rome

98 *Self-Portrait*. 1940. 15¾ × 11¾″. Private collection, Rome

99 *Horses in the Forest*. 1958. 19⅝ × 23⅝″. Private collection, Rome

100 *Roger and Angelica*. 1950. 59 × 39⅜″. Private collection, Rome

101 *Roger and Angelica*. 1950. 59 × 39⅜″. Private collection, Rome

102 *Peaches*. 1965. 11¾ × 15¾″. Private collection, Rome

103 *Grapes and Rocks*. 1944. 13¾ × 17¾″. Private collection, Rome

104 *Lucretia*. 1922. 66⅞ × 29⅛″. Private collection, Rome

105 *Perseus and Andromeda*. 1940. 35⅜ × 46½″. Private collection, Rome

106 *Landscape with Horses*. 1954. Lithograph. Private collection, Rome

107 *The Departure of the Knight Errant*. 1921–24. 19¼ × 26⅜″. Private collection, Rome

108 *Greek Youth Taming a Horse*. 1954. 24⅜ × 31⅛″. Private collection, Rome

109 *Hector with One of His Horses*. 1961. 24⅜ × 31⅛″. Private collection, Rome

110 *Still Life with Bust of Apollo*. 1962. 39⅜ × 55⅛″. Collection Isabella Far, Rome

111 *Landscape with Castle*. 1956. 12⅝ × 16½″. Private collection, Rome

112 *Landscape with Horses*. 1954. 11¾ × 15¾″. Private collection, Rome

113 *Still Life*. 1948. 11¾ × 17⅜″. Private collection, Rome

114 *Self-Portrait in the Costume of an Eighteenth-Century Gentleman*. 1954. 29½ × 24⅜″. Private collection, Rome

115 *Portrait of a Young Italian Woman*. 1948. 35 × 33½″. Private collection, Rome

116 *Doge's Palace*. 1955. 23⅝ × 31½″. Private collection, Rome

117 *Pomegranates*. 1946. 7⅛ × 12⅝″. Private collection, Rome

118 *Phrygian Horseman*. 1936. 22 × 12⅝″. Private collection, Rome

119 *The Gladiators*. 1954. 39⅜ × 31½″. Private collection, Rome

120 *The School of the Amazons*. 1936. 31½ × 39⅜″. Collection Max Perl, New York

121 *Self-Portrait with Head of Minerva*. 1957. 31½ × 23⅝″. Private collection, Rome

122 *Horses in the Sunset*. 1956. 19⅝ × 23⅝″. Private collection, Rome

123 Stage Design for Boïto's *Mefistofele*. 1951–52. 11¾ × 15¾″. La Scala, Milan

124 Stage Design for *Mefistofele*. 1951–52. 15¾ × 11¾″. La Scala, Milan

125 Stage Design for *Mefistofele*. 1951–52. 11¾ × 15¾″. La Scala, Milan

126 Drop-curtain Design for Richard Strauss's *Josefslegende*. 1951–52. 11¾ × 15¾″. La Scala, Milan

127 *Portrait of the Artist's Mother*. 1911. 33⅛ × 23⅝″. Private collection, Rome

128 *Bust of Minerva*. 1942. 23⅝ × 19⅝″. Private collection, Rome

129 *Temple in a Room*. 1927. 19⅝ × 23⅝″. Private collection, Rome

130 *Phaetusan Nymph on the Island of Trinacria (Sicily)*. 1945. 42½ × 33½″. Private collection, Rome

131 *The Repose of Alcmene*. 1933. 29½ × 55⅛″. Private collection, Rome

132 *Portrait of Isabella Far in Seventeenth-Century Costume*. 1956. 59 × 38⅝″. Private collection, Rome

133 *Self-Portrait in Seventeenth-Century Costume*. 1953. 59 × 39⅜″. Private collection, Rome

134 *Divine Horses of Achilles: Balios and Xanthos.* 1963. 39⅜ × 33½". Collection Isabella Far, Rome

135 *Ancient Horses.* 1961. 31½ × 23⅝". Private collection, Rome

136 *Achilles.* 1952. 11 × 7½". Private collection, Rome

137 *Three Graces.* 1951. 43¼ × 43¼". Private collection, Rome

138 *Self-Portrait in Costume.* 1959. 60¼ × 38⅝". Private collection, Rome .

139 *Historical Regattas at Venice.* 1952. 31½ × 47¼". Private collection, Rome

140 *Nude Self-Portrait.* 1942. 23⅝ × 19¼". Private collection, Rome

141 *Ephebe with Horse.* 1935. 17⅜ × 13¾". Private collection, Rome

142 *The Baron's Promenade.* 1957. 13⅜ × 8⅝". Collection Isabella Far, Rome

143 *Fish.* 1959. 19⅝ × 27⅝". Collection Umberto Lombardi, Florence

144 *Fruit.* 1932. 31½ × 55⅛". Private collection, Rome

145 *Ancient Horses.* 1965. 31½ × 23⅝". Private collection, Rome

146 Stage Design for Bellini's *I Puritani.* 1934. 24½ × 40⅛". Private collection, Rome

147 *Self-Portrait.* 1943. 19⅝ × 15¾". Private collection, Rome

148 *Hat with Plumes.* 1954. 23⅝ × 19⅝". Private collection, Rome

149 *Standing Figure.* 1937. Drawing. Private collection, Rome

150 *The Gladiators.* 1958. 23⅝ × 19⅝". Private collection, Rome

151 *The Enchanted Forest.* 1953. 19⅝ × 23⅝". Private collection, Rome

152 *Villa Falconieri.* 1942. 15¾ × 19⅝". Private collection, Rome

153 *Sunlight in a Room.* 1966. 23⅝ × 19⅝". Private collection, Rome

154 *Sunlight on an Easel.* 1966. 23⅝ × 19⅝". Private collection, Rome

155 *Sibyl.* 1940. 14⅝ × 10⅝". Private collection, Rome

156 *The Return from Troy.* 1966. 15¾ × 19⅝". Private collection, Rome

157 *Fruit.* 1955. 7⅞ × 11¾". Private collection, Rome

158 *Bacchus* (autumnal allegory after Rubens). 1953. 15¾ × 11¾". Private collection, Rome

159 *Phaetusan Nymphs.* 1947. 9½ × 19½". Private collection, Rome

160 *Dioscuri.* 1943. 43¼ × 57⅛". Private collection, Rome

161 *Bather.* 1933. 43¼ × 59". Private collection, Rome

162 *Grapes and Apple.* 1943. 12¼ × 17¾". Private collection, Rome

163 *Portrait with the Bust of Minerva.* 1942. 19⅝ × 24¾". Private collection, Rome

164 *The Island of San Giorgio.* 1943. 23⅝ × 19⅝". Private collection, Rome

165 *Roman Landscape with Horsemen.* 1946. 37⅜ × 53⅛". Private collection, Rome

166 *Sleeping Woman.* 1934. 14⅛ × 16⅞". Private collection, Rome

167 *Self-Portrait in Seventeenth-Century Costume.* 1949. 31½ × 22⅞". Private collection, Rome

168 *The Naiads.* 1955. 15¾ × 11¾". Private collection, Rome

169 *Nude.* 1930. 25⅝ × 21⅝". Collection Umberto Lombardi, Florence

170 *Hat with Plumes.* 1939. Drawing. Private collection

171 *The Two Friends.* 1940. Collection Isabella Far, Rome

172 *Self-Portrait.* 1957. 19⅝ × 15¾". Private collection, Rome

(21

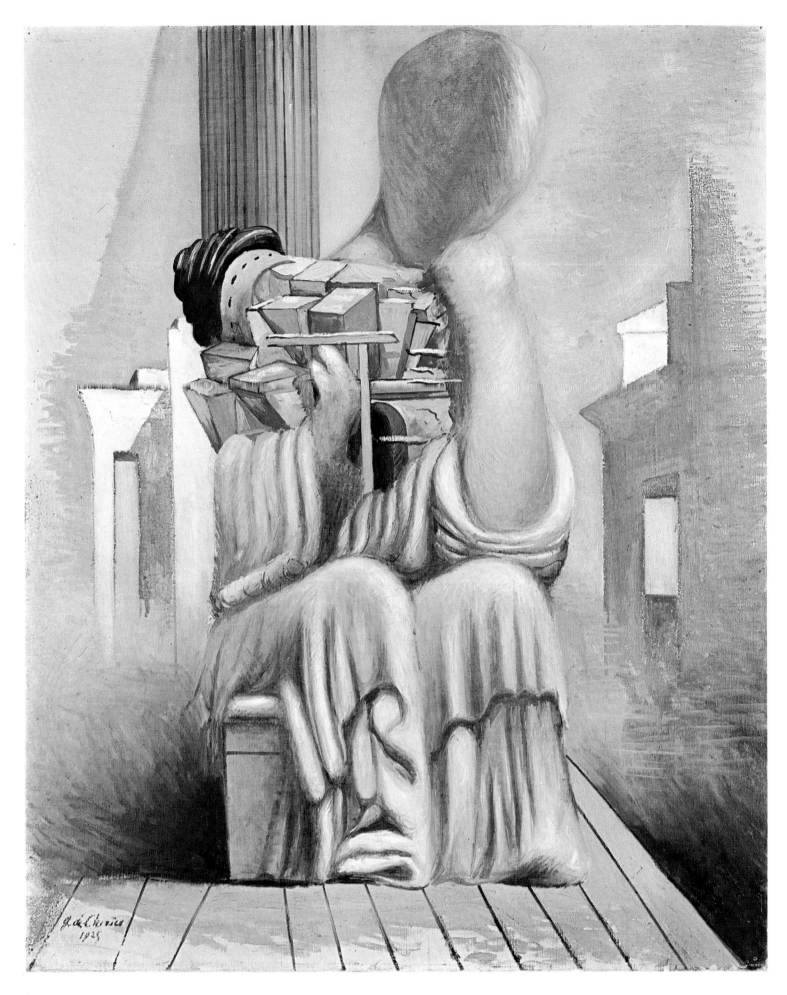

1

2

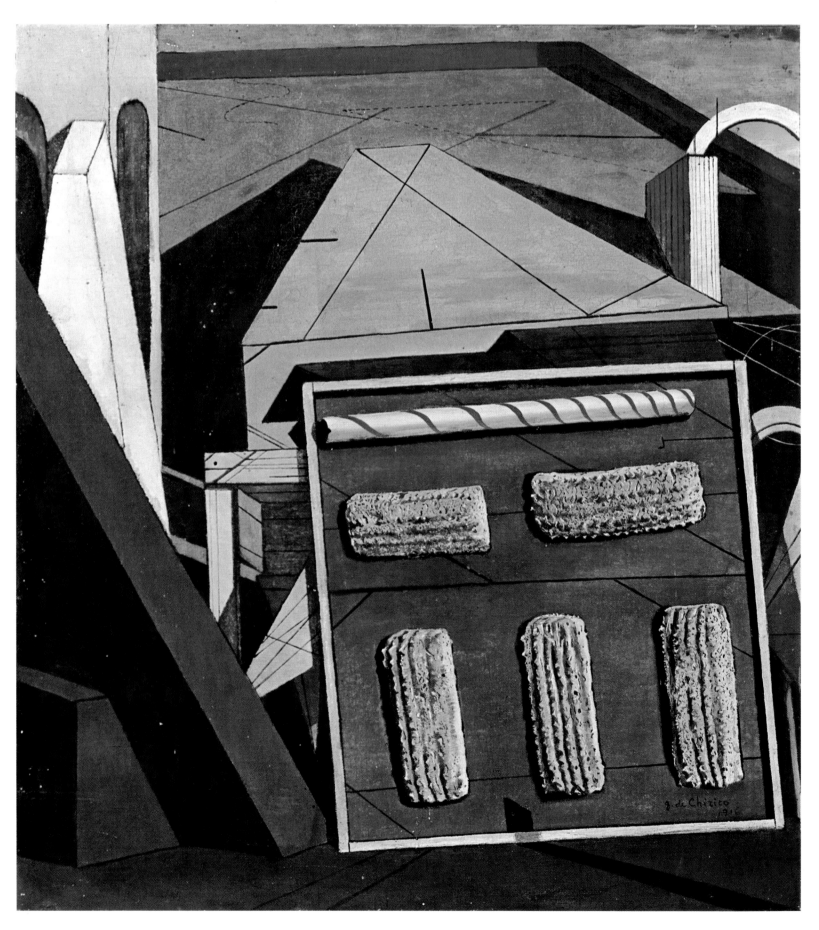

4

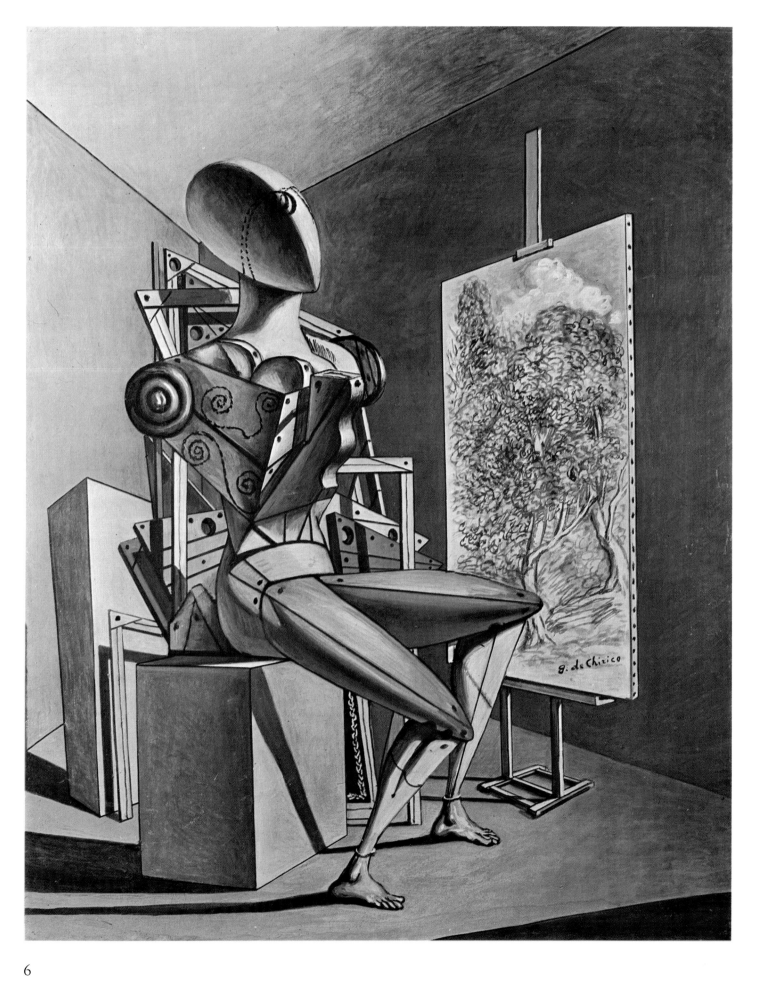

8

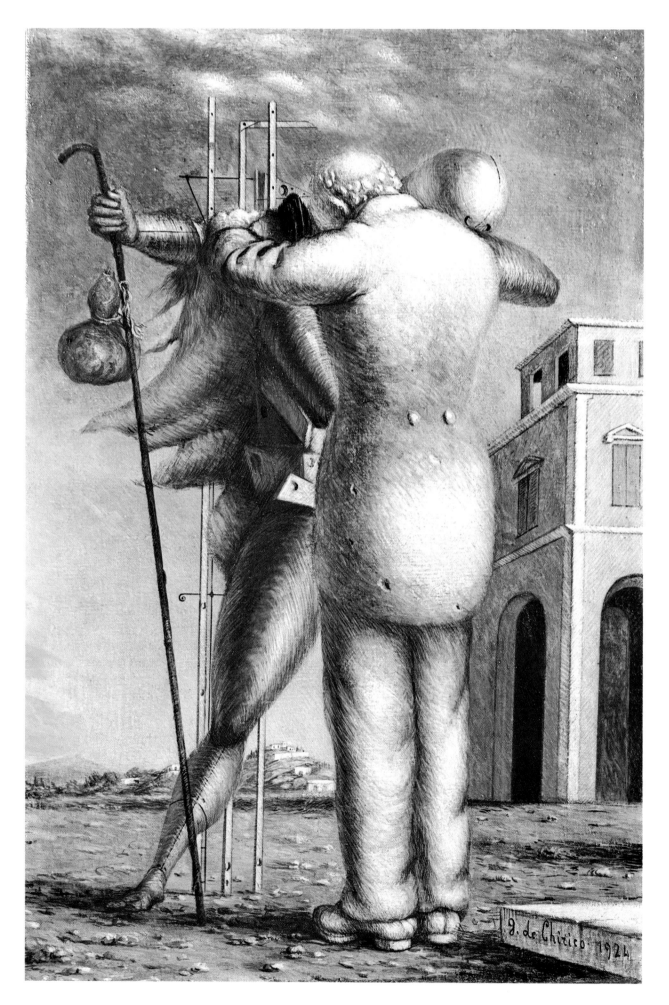

9

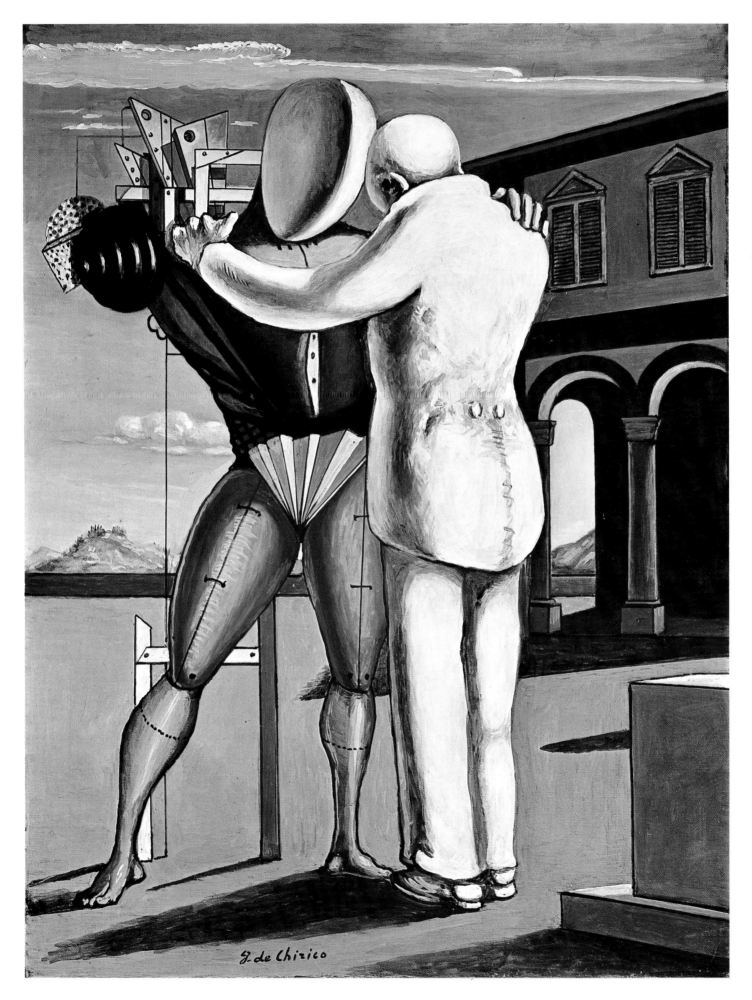

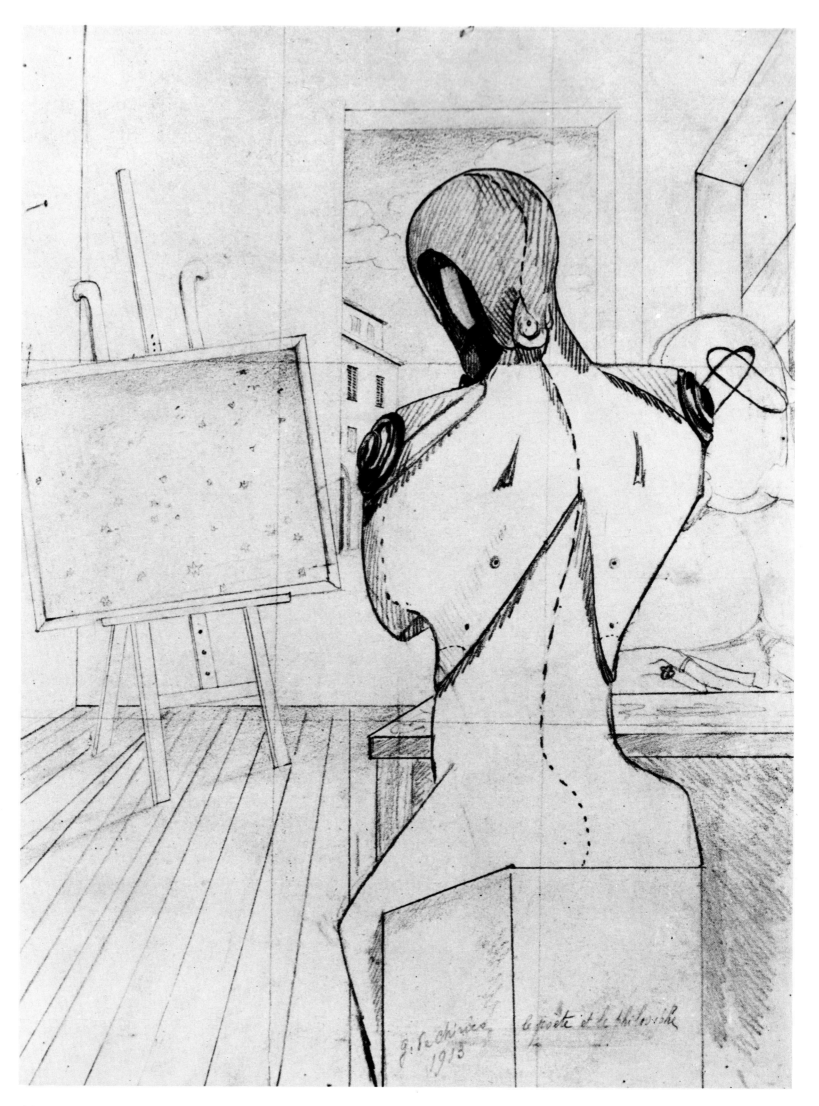

12

13

14

15

16

17

La Joie

19

20

21

24

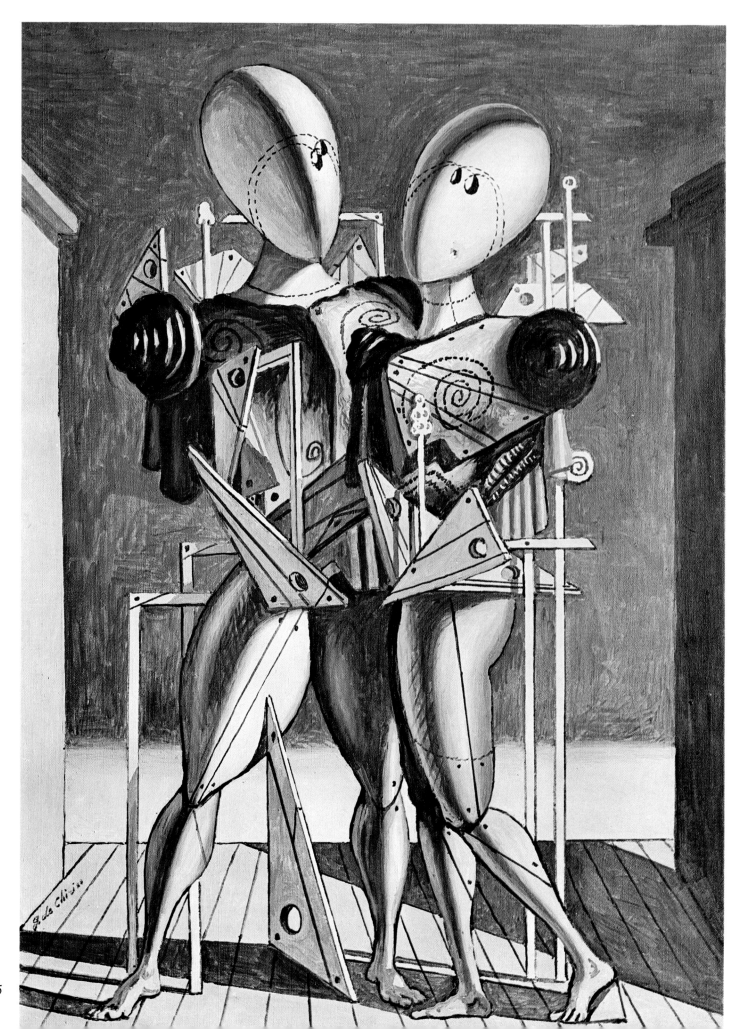

26

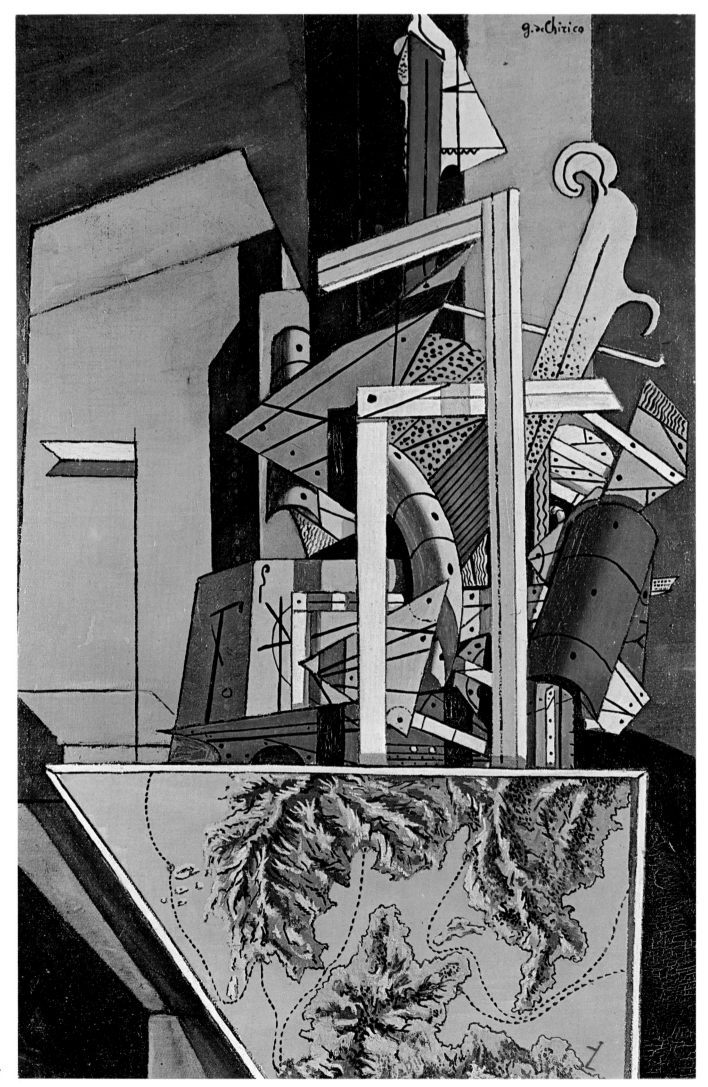

28

31

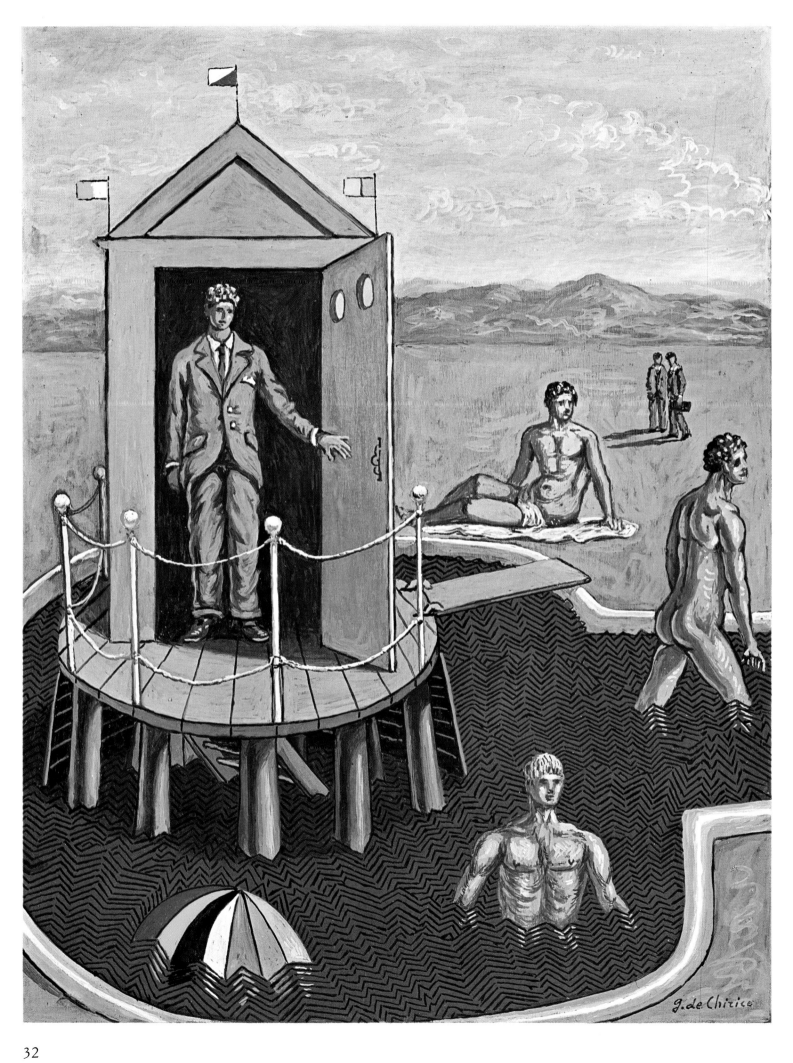

35

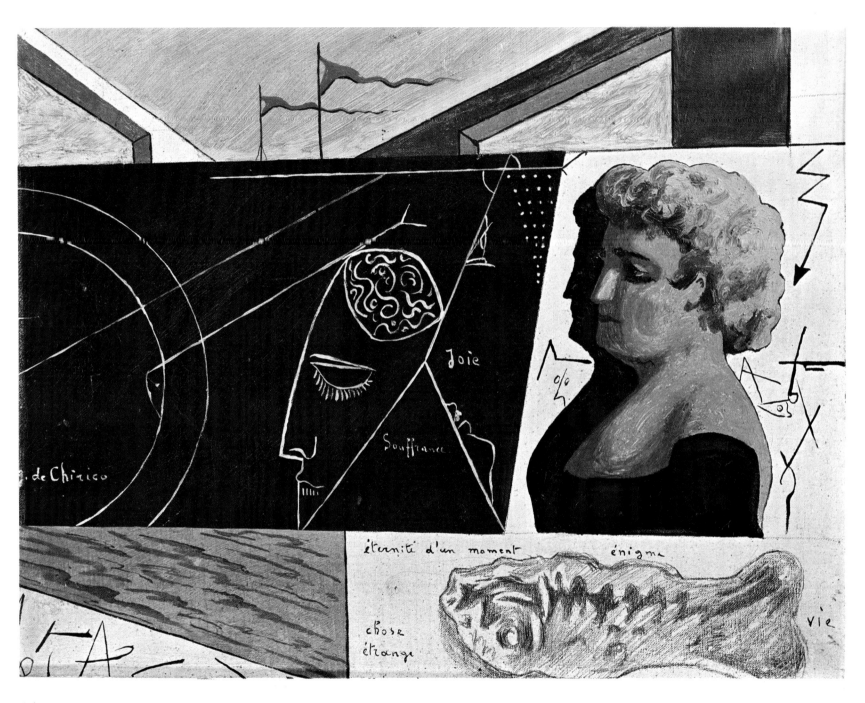

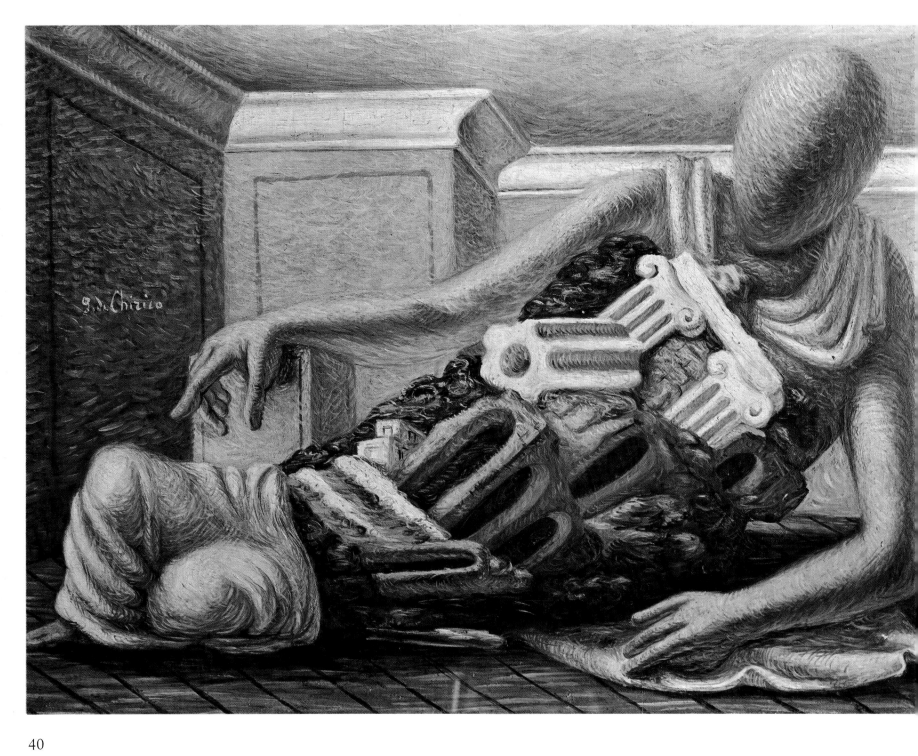

40

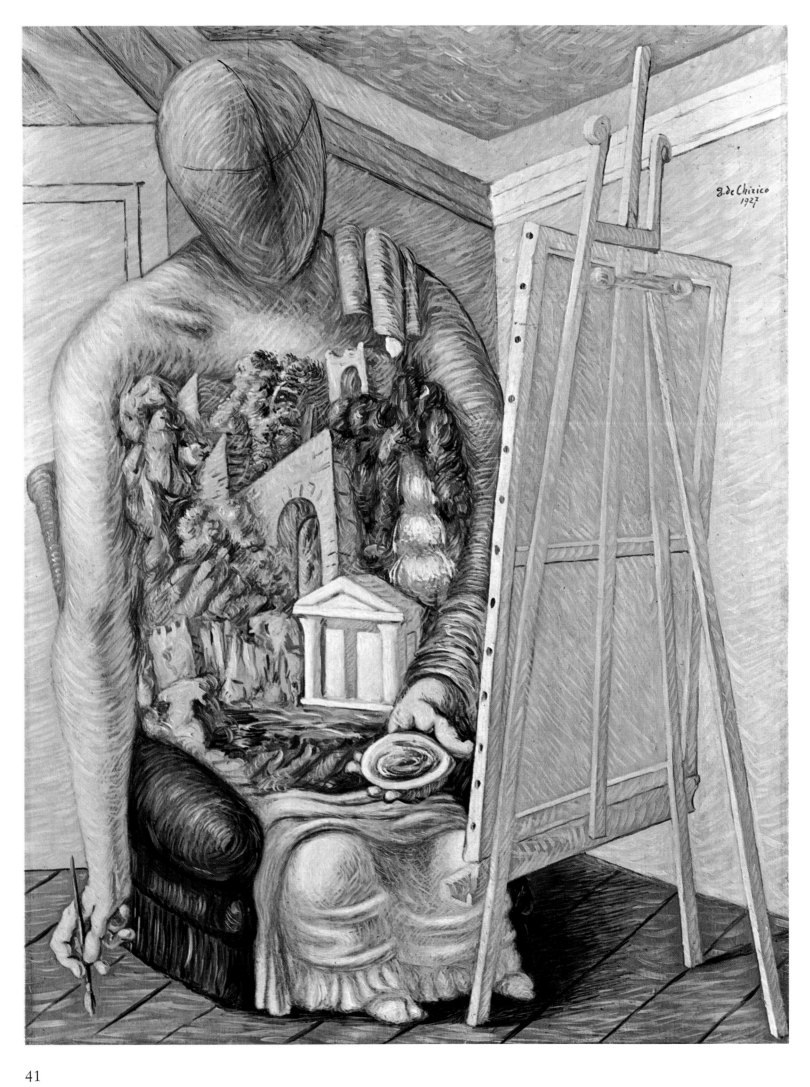

41

42

45

47

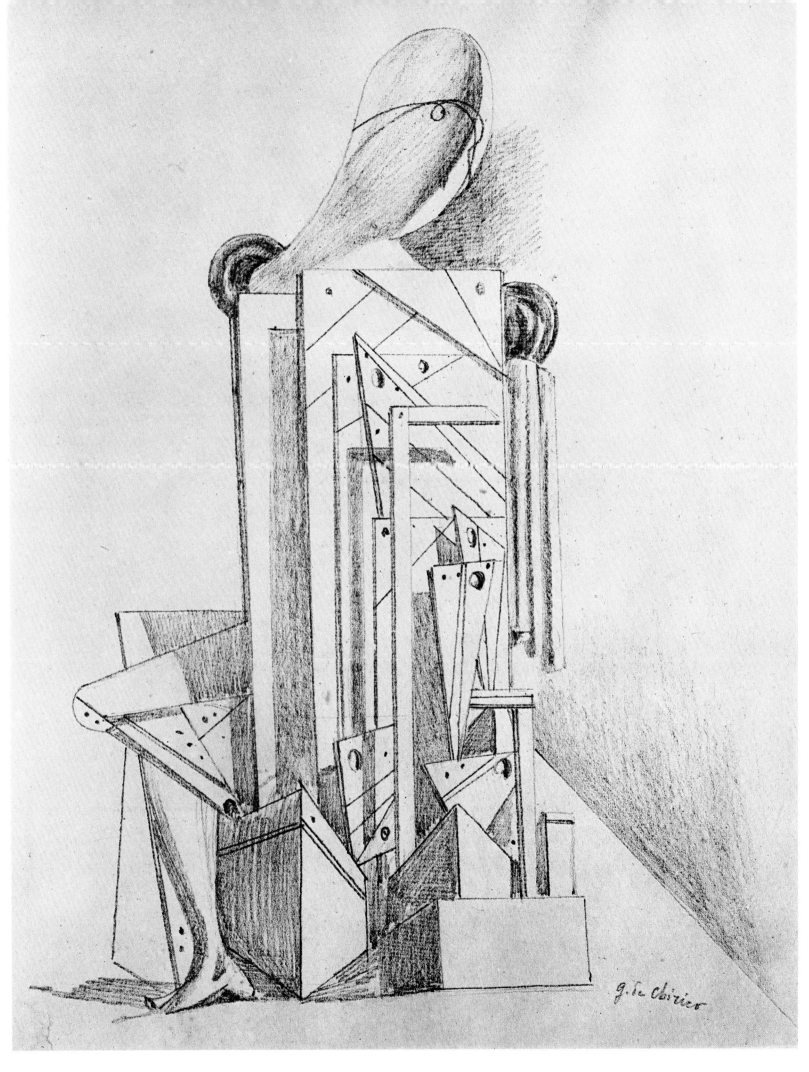

48

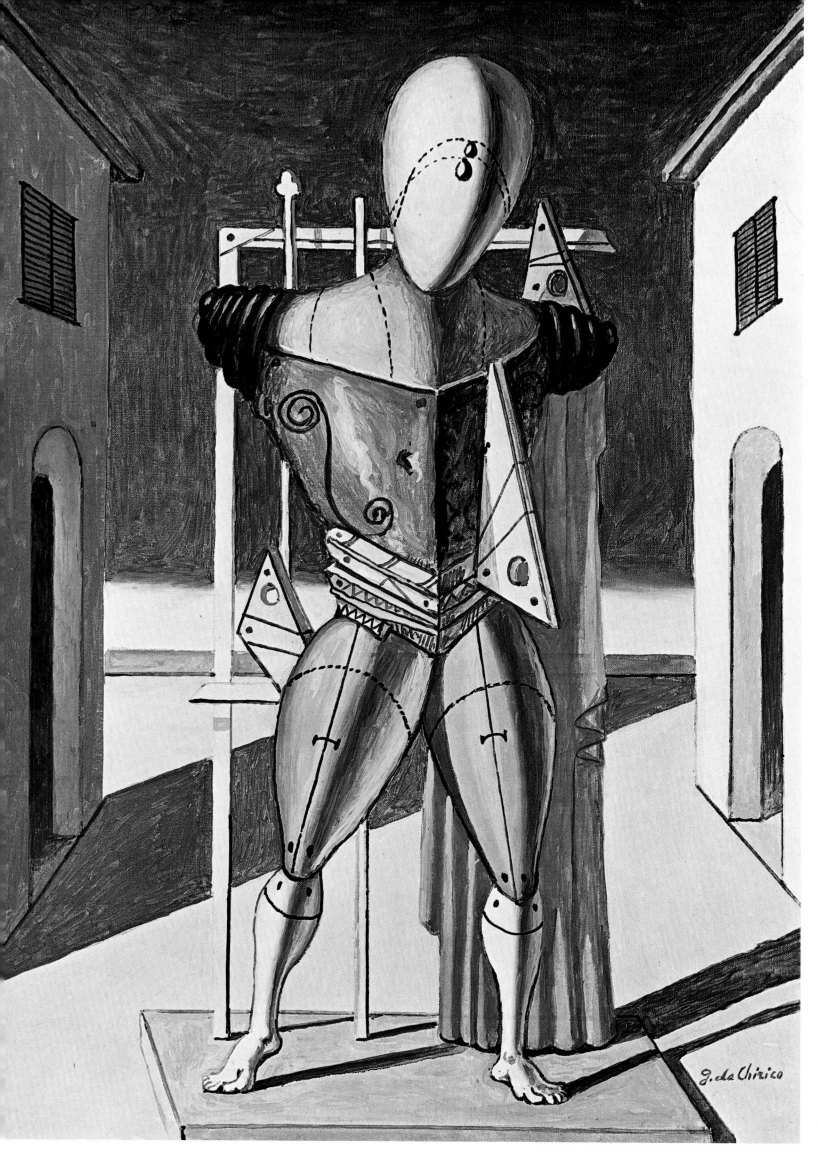

51

52

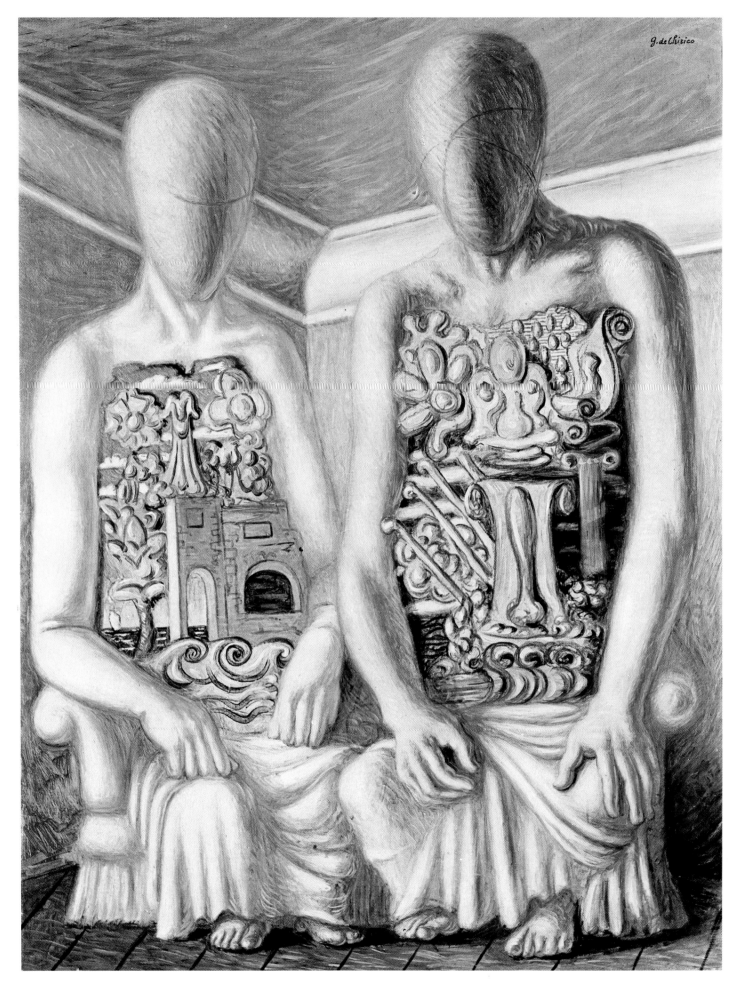

54

57

58

9

61

62

64

65

66

69

71

72

73

75

78

82

g. de Chirico

83

84

89

91

92

93

94

96

97

101

102

103

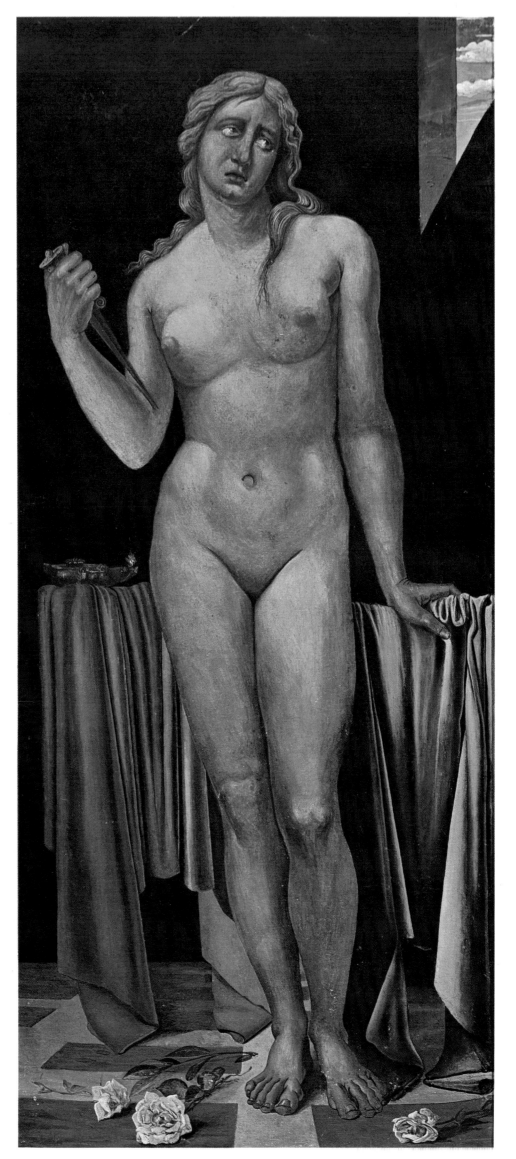

104

105

106

108

109

111

112

113

114

115

g. de Chirico

16

117

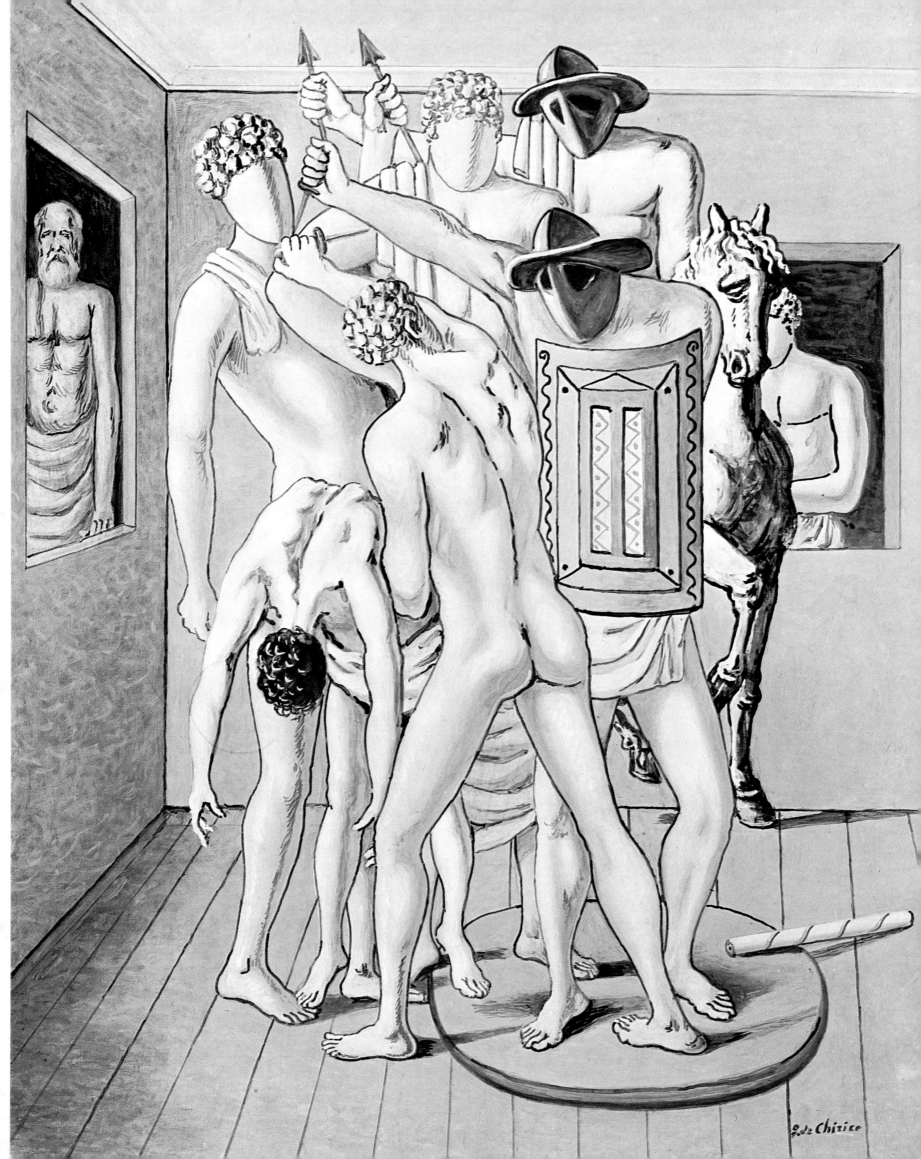

122

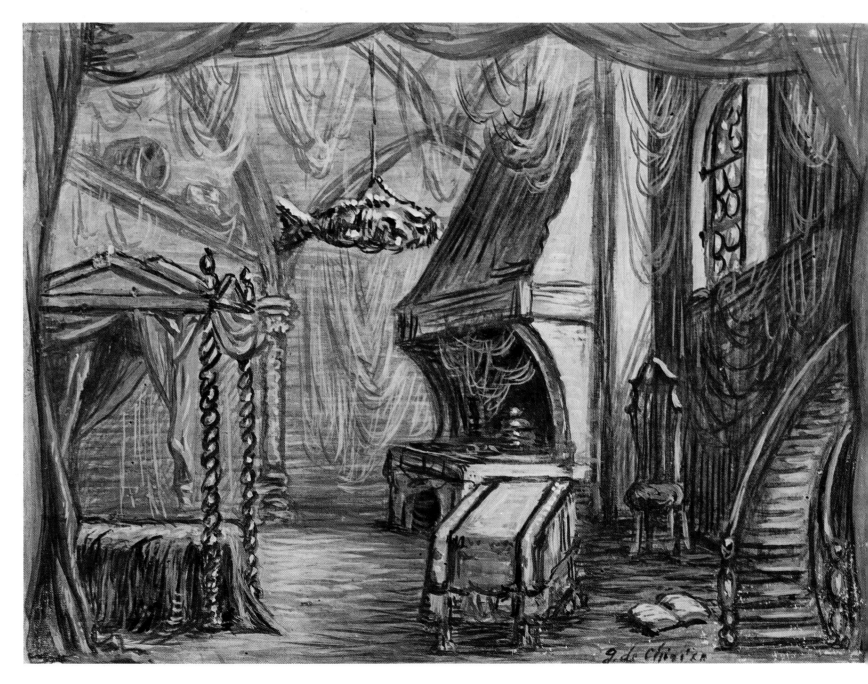

123

g. de Chirico

125

129

130

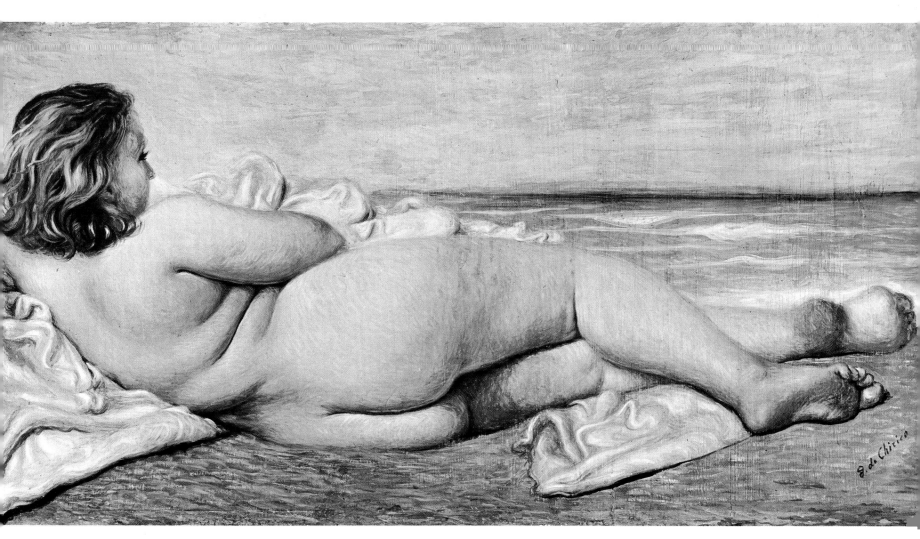

131

132

133

137

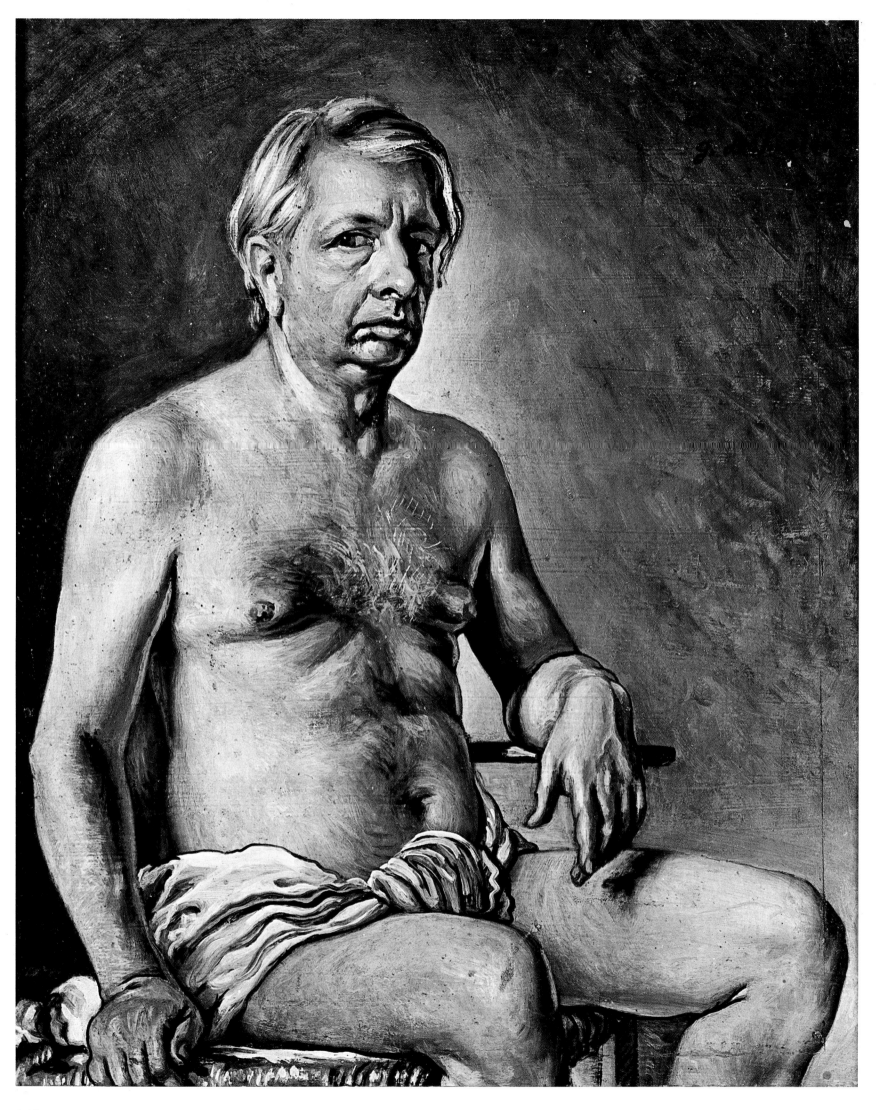

141

142

143

144

145

146

147

148

149

150

151

52

153

154

157

158

159

160

51

162

163

164

165

166

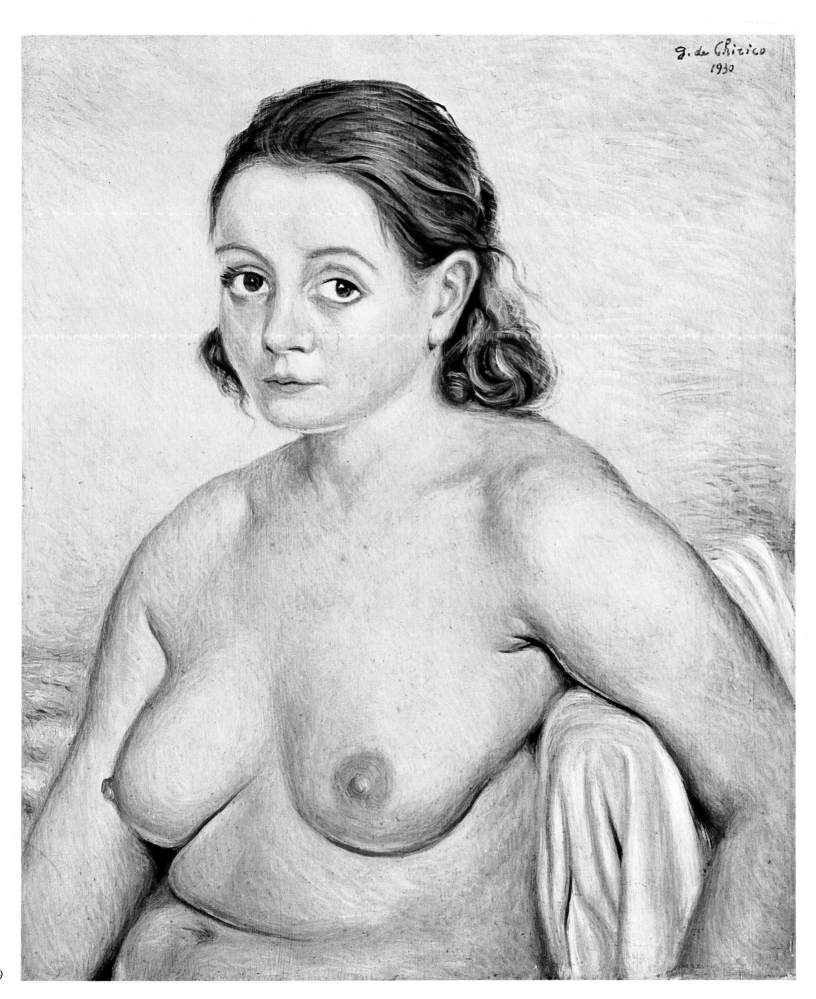

169

170

71

172